A Living Light

A Living Light

E. L. Risden

WIPF & STOCK · Eugene, Oregon

A LIVING LIGHT

Copyright © 2009 E. L. Risden. All rights reserved. Except for brief quotations in critical publications or reviews, no part of this book may be reproduced in any manner without prior written permission from the publisher. Write: Permissions, Wipf and Stock Publishers, 199 W. 8th Ave., Suite 3, Eugene, OR 97401.

Wipf & Stock
A Division of Wipf and Stock Publishers
199 W. 8th Ave., Suite 3
Eugene, OR 97401

www.wipfandstock.com

ISBN 13: 978-160608-091-7

Manufactured in the U.S.A.

Contents

Acknowledgments vii
Introduction ix
List of Characters xvii

Chapter One 1

Chapter Two 35

Chapter Three 77

Hildegard's Writings 121
Selected Secondary Bibliography 123

Acknowledgments

THANKS TO Professor Kelly Collum and all the students, staff, and community members who debuted this work in dramatic form in November of 1992. Thanks also to Professor Bruce Hozeski of Ball State University, who made space for a fiction reading in the joint conference of the Committee for the Advancement of Early Studies and the Hildegard Society at Muncie, Indiana, in October 2002. Thanks finally to all the excellent scholars whose work informed this project and to Wipf and Stock for bringing it at last to print.

Introduction

Hildegard of Bingen

LOOKING BACK at the Middle Ages with the scholarly perspective of several hundred years, we may reasonably call Hildegard of Bingen—abbess, mystic, physician, poet, musician, exorcist, political activist, and devoted servant of God and humanity–one of the foremost intellectuals of her time. Her abilities and influence touched popes and kings, and the work that she left us shows heart and soul mingled with vision, keen observation, knowledge of theology and natural history, and simple hard work.

Hildegard was born in 1098 in Bermersheim, not far from Mainz, in western Germany, the tenth child of a noble family. At eight years of age she was "tithed" to God by her parents, that is, given as the tenth of their possessions owed the Church. She entered a cloister that was attached to a monastery at nearby Disibodenberg, where she trained under an accomplished anchoress named Jutta. When Jutta died, Hildegard became abbess of the growing community of nuns. She eventually moved her charges to a new convent at nearby Rupertsberg, on a hill above the Rhine (ca. 1150). Later, she founded a second convent at Eibingen. Though she had visions even as a child, not until her forty-third year, during an illness, when she received a vision commanding her to write what she had been seeing and hearing, did she begin to record her mystical experiences. Her first book,

Scivias ("Know the Ways [of the Lord])" details those visions, and its approval by Pope Eugenius (ca. 1148) assured Hildegard the opportunity to continue and expand her efforts in preaching and healing as well as her right to preserve her visions with impunity. Her later writings include the *Ordo Virtutum*, a kind of medieval opera in praise of the cardinal virtues, books on medicine and natural philosophy, two other visionary works, plus some poetry, biography, commentary, and a substantial correspondence.

Accompanying her mystical works are marvelous illuminations, probably not made by Hildegard herself, but certainly done according to her direction. The originality and power of these textual illustrations represent a contribution to the history of art as well as to mysticism and theology. In addition to several preaching tours, Hildegard undertook regularly to meet with and treat a great number of pilgrims who came to her for advice, medicine, or simply to share prayer. Legend has it that "two streams of light crossed over the room" (Fox, Introduction to *Scivias*, 11) in which she died in 1179; she had lived quite a long and influential life for someone of that time. Although the Church has never officially canonized her, she was beatified, and so she is known to most readers and scholars as St. Hildegard. Within the past twenty years Hildegard scholarship has become a small but productive industry, and books and web pages have sprung up providing access particularly to her illuminated writings and music. Scholarly organizations, such as the International Society of Hildegard von Bingen Studies, meet regularly to discuss her accomplishments and advance understanding of her spiritual, artistic, and intellectual contributions. Her gifts to our age increase as our appreciation and familiarity grow.

The Novella

A Living Light compacts several major events in Hildegard's life during the twelfth century into a brief span of time appropriate to dramatic presentation. Those events include the approval of her work by the Trier Synod, her forming a new convent at Rupertsberg, the death of her secretary and friend Volmar, the departure and subsequent death of her friend and colleague Richardis, and the disputed burial of an accused criminal on convent grounds, followed by the subsequent interdiction (denial of the sacraments) imposed briefly on her convent. Despite a long and what must have been for a medieval nun eventful life, Hildegard's story requires some editing and some enhancing for fictionalization. I have allowed myself freedom to choose and telescope events and condense time so as to show the essential character of the protagonist and give readers a sense of her personality and struggles, rather than sticking exactly to the time line of her life. I have varied events where I thought dramatically necessary: for instance, I have no reason to believe that Abbot Kuno was the choleric antagonist that I portray, and scholars suggest that Richardis, one of Hildegard's nuns, left by her choice to found her own convent, rather than compelled by her family as I have depicted. What you are about to read is thoroughly fiction, not a scholarly disquisition, though I owe considerable debt to the work of several excellent scholars, particularly Profs. Bruce Hozeski and Sabina Flanagan. Their books I have noted in a brief bibliography, along with others that have especially helped me, following the text of the novel: without the work of those and many other scholars, I could not have written this book.

The purpose of the story is to show Hildegard's (and her world's) struggle with her visions and their power and to get a sense of what they may mean to us in our own lives. It focuses on the doubt and the religious, social, and physical difficulties a medieval visionary would have suffered. I aimed foremost to consider her personality and how she may have dealt with the doubts that any of us in her position might face. She represents, allegorically, a point I find important to any age, the individual's engagement with personal spirituality. Other characters, while most represent actual historical persons, dramatically represent aspects of Hildegard's personality or some resistance she would have met to following her calling in an age in which some men weren't willing to admit even that women have souls. Some characters I have simplified, some amplified, and some created. Sister Keunegard, for instance, is not an actual person: she crept into the story as I wrote it, and she illustrates how many men may have seen Hildegard or what Hildegard might have done had she been mentally ill rather than a true mystic. The rustics should look familiar to all readers of Greek or Elizabethan drama as enactors of or commentators on the situations of the story and the time in which the story occurs. As for Hildegard's visions, some scholars have suggested that they may have come more from migraine headaches rather than from actual mystical experience; I have based my novel on the premise that, whatever the cause, Hildegard's visions display a mystical truth valid for us as it was for her believing contemporaries. I have structured chapters and scenes also so that they reflect and balance one another, so that one may comment on another, much after the fashion of a Shakespeare play. The progress of the story shows the mystic's difficulties in balancing heavenly vision with the hard work of daily, earthly duties. The visions related in the story come, with slight variations, from the texts that record Hildegard's recitations of them. My greatest hope for this story is that it will spur additional interest in Hildegard, in her times, and in many like her who have not always received accolades but who have contributed to our spiritual, social, and intellectual growth.

I tried to write this story not only as an exploration of character, but also as an expedition into the twelfth century mindset. The reader may at first find the dialogue a bit heightened and distant, but my experience suggests that such problems can turn to pleasure if one gets caught up in the world of the text. The language itself becomes a character, and I intend it to suggest a world rather different from ours in belief structure as well as time and place, but exhibiting many of our hopes and worries: a thoroughly spiritual world more tightly circumscribed. The action of the story takes place over perhaps several weeks; I hope my adjustment of historical timing will help the reader follow a psychological necessity with respect to where the action is taking place and how events connect to those past and those to come. The project began as a stage play. The premier of the play at St. Norbert College in November of 1992 was done, as I had hoped, in a very classical or Shakespearean fashion, with the focus on character interaction. A small theater with unusual capacity for effects allowed for some interesting experiments with lighting and staging and with projecting images similar to the illuminations from Hildegard's texts on backdrops or parts of the stage either between acts or during the actual performance, so as to throw more symbolic weight on characters' entrances and exits. The performance of the first production took about two and a half hours, including two brief intermissions between acts. To turn the play into a novella I have added connective matter and description, but have cut little dialogue and have largely kept the dialogue-based format; I have added a couple more of Hildegard's visions, but have tried to keep the hypotactic movement characteristic of drama. I have kept the story short so that one may read it in a period of time not far beyond the length of a typical play or movie, aiming for intensity rather than breadth and for a focus on character rather than on description–the preference of many if not most readers of our time.

Historical Context

The eleventh and twelfth Centuries saw a great deal of change in the relationship between Church and lay authorities. In the mid-eleventh century the Holy Roman Empire and its German king controlled the papacy and most Church appointments, and churchmen often served in secular administrative capacities. Simony, the buying and selling of Church offices, occurred commonly. In the second half of the century a reform movement began, first to eliminate clerical abuses, but later to reverse the governmental order, so that secular governors fell subject to the Church and even kings subordinate to the Pope. Signs suggested that internal strife within the empire might break it up into separate kingdoms, until the excommunicated emperor Henry IV, in a difficult if politically astute move, submitted to Pope Gregory VII and begged forgiveness for having tried to wrest authority from his hands. Having thus restored his political position amidst a pious nobility, Henry set about to re-establish his influence and ultimately brought about Gregory's fall from the papacy. Pope Urban II restored lost political clout to the papacy not only by calling for the First Crusade, but also by gradually undermining Henry's authority. With the succession of Henry IV's son, Henry V, an unstable balance developed between Church and state that would continue until, and even after, the dissolution of the empire. A generation later Frederick Barbarossa set about to restore imperial power, and after a back-and-forth struggle with Pope Alexander III, ultimately managed a firm-handed rule of Germany until his death while leading an army during the Third Crusade, in 1190. One must wonder if the continual struggle between ecclesiastical and secular authority did not provide the perfect opportunity for Hildegard to gain influence both among the powerful and among the common, since all were searching for means to understand, deal with, and even perhaps master the constantly changing circumstances. Hildegard's voice rises above the confusion as one of piety, sanity, and even, somewhat oddly for her time and place, individuality.

Intellectually the twelfth century experienced a pre-renaissance, largely because of the circulation of Classical learning that the West had lost long before, but that it rediscovered through the Crusades and the Christian Reconquest of Spain: the Arabs had preserved Greek manuscripts and had added considerably to what the Greeks had accomplished. Expanded knowledge especially of the works of Aristotle led in the next century to Scholasticism, but already the Twelfth had begun to rely more on reason and empirical discovery than had the West since before the Fall of Rome. Arabic scholars had made particular advancements in mathematics, science, and medicine, and though the Europeans discarded neither all of their old vernacular learning nor their attachment to "magic," they did benefit from the influx of knowledge and the expanding sense of the world that came with it. Such a climate would not have delivered Hildegard or others in similar walks of life to absolutely free expression, but it would at least have encouraged a greater number of her contemporaries to read, write, think, and communicate their thoughts to others, and it would have given them a rather larger understanding of the world.

While women had nominally little power, they would have had a greater likelihood in Hildegard's time of gaining some education, and some noblewomen would have directed estates when their lords were off fighting in Crusades. By the end of the century we see the emergence of at least one important female literary figure, Marie de France, who, though she wrote secular tales, showed what a woman could accomplish given her opportunity to explore her voice. We find in Hildegard's work nothing of secular Romance or commerce, but we do find, once she frees herself from a reluctance to speak, eagerness to share her visions, knowledge, artistic output, medical wisdom, and political opinion.

While Hildegard lived a century and a half before the first stirrings of the Renaissance proper, artistically and intellectually her age saw the building of the great Gothic cathedrals such as that at Chartres and the opening of the first universities, and it knew characters who have left lasting impressions on the world: Thomas á Beckett, St. Bernard, Abelard and Heloise, Marie de France, and Chretien de Troyes.

A Living Light

A Historical Novella in Three Chapters,
Based on the Life of Hildegard of Bingen

Characters

Hildegard of Bingen, an abbess
Richardis, a nun and Hildegard's confidant
Clementia, a nun
Irmengard, a nun
Keunegard, a nun
Sigewize, a mad girl
Adelheid, a nun
Kuno, Abbot at Disibodenberg
Volmar, a monk and Hildegard's secretary
Guibert, a monk
Pope Eugenius
Henry, Archbishop of Mainz
Bernard of Clairvaux
Herman, Bishop of Constance
Hartwig, Archbishop of Bremen (Richardis's brother)
Marchioness of Stade (Ricardis's mother)
Spirit of Jutta, Hildegard's deceased abbess
Frederick Barbarossa
Datta, Dayadva, Damyata, Dall, and Donau, entertainers
Rache, a revolutionary
Fear-of-God, a figure in a vision
Assorted nuns, priests, monks, soldiers, and folk

Chapter One

In the midst of a synod in Rome, around the middle of the twelfth century, the Pope met with a number of his trusted counselors to consider the matter of a German nun: her visions, her outspokenness, her effect on the flock. Once obscure, she had risen to prominence and even popularity among the people by her piety and through the vehemence and magnitude of her visions—as well as through her skill in healing and her ability to help people with their daily problems. Her current exposure, all the way to the the apex of Church power, placed at risk her public and private voice and perhaps even her life, but she had no choice: she lived at and for the will of the Church, at and for the will of God. The voices of the council, grave and formal as they discussed her case, buzzed in the warm Italian air.

Such review, common enough, had found for once an uncommon subject, the writings of one Hildegard of Bingen, abbess and mystic. Pope Eugenius called not only his usual advisors, but also representatives of her own region and in fact her own secretary, who had seen her in the full flight of recounting her visions for him to record: Volmar, monk and scribe, served devotedly, recording her speech with accuracy and awe. A papal scribe (no manuscript records his name) recorded testimony as men of power, learning, and experience argued the fate of the learned nun, yet little known to the wide world, but loved among her folk. Some of the men sipped Tuscan wine. The Pope drank nothing, not even cool water, which he knew would have done him good: he wanted his thoughts fixed and precise. Volmar scratched his tonsure and drank several bowls of water as the discussion continued and as he knew his time to speak drew near. The Pope's stern forehead and impassive, almost charcoal-grey eyes intimidated the monk, but something affable about the mouth made him feel eager to speak. He tried to calm himself to wait his turn.

> Eugenius: Enlighten us to your opinion, Constance.
>
> Herman: I have indeed sought her prayers, Eminence. She is as well known for their efficacy as for that of her medicines, which, though we value the less, draw the more worldly of her flock. And yet I fear to give too quick credence to these wild visions.
>
> Eugenius: And you, Mainz: fair or fulsome?
>
> Henry: Sincerity scatters like moths at the dawn, your Holiness, and yet I think her sincere. The visions seem to come conveniently, when she desires what the vision confirms, and yet I believe them from God.
>
> Volmar: Visions, Holy Father, visions that spark joyous as a greenwood fire on the Christmas hearth, youthful as spring and ancient as air, dancing as mayday children yet somber as final unction.
>
> Eugenius: Please, my son, we will hear you, but let us defer first to your father the abbot.
>
> Volmar: Apologies, your Holiness.
>
> Eugenius: She has been in your charge many years, Abbot. What then do you see in these visions, our dear Kuno? Have you not compassed her training?
>
> Kuno: In truth, My Lord, neither drawn nor circled it. She is a willful one, given more to flowers, trance, and parchment than hours and office.

Chapter One 3

Eugenius: Has she failed in her duties or offended?

Kuno: Not so much failed or offended as strayed from a sister's truer course, that of quiet, unobtrusive obedience. The folk flock to her, write to her . . .

Herman and Henry: So we have.

Kuno: . . . call her name in the towns, and for herself, she will fall into a fit or lingering humor until her latest fancy is dictated word for word for posterity.

Volmar: But her words, Holy Father, or rather God's words through her, have such truth and power!

Herman: This council shall determine that.

Eugenius: We have reviewed much of her book, but we would hear more. If you please, Our Son, read to us and let the words speak, that we may judge whence they come.

Volmar: Gladly, Holiness. "Behold, in the forty-third year of my journey I saw a living light, from which heaven's voice spoke to me, saying 'Weak one of ashes, dust of dust, decay of decay, tell and write what you see and hear. Because you are simple and timid, do not speak according to the words of humans, but listen and tell plainly the wonder of God according to the words of God.'" (He thumbed through pages.) And later she tells, "Then I saw a multitude of living torches and, beneath, a wide lake deep as the mouth of a well that billowed forth clouds of smoke that climbed, till out of them fell like a shooting star the figure of a man into the smoking depths, and the heavens were brightened again, but the earth trembled."

Herman: Surely that means Satan!

Volmar: And again later: "And then I saw a huge egg, encircled by flame, and within the egg a fire-red globe, and above the globe torches that kept the flame from burning the globe to ashes, and the globe would rise and fall toward the willing flame above or sink toward gloomy fire below."

Herman: God and Satan calling the souls of the earth, and the saints interceding.

Volmar: "And next I saw a great, peaceful brightness full of eyes turned toward all the four corners of the world and, within, a purple lightening brightening the way for those who carried milk and bread and cheese, and among the folk a woman carrying a child inside her, and the brightness, from its own heart, reached within her, quickening the child from the womb."

Herman: That is God bringing Christ to the world.

Eugenius: I see, Bishop, that you are as taken with these visions as I am.

Henry: And I, am, too, Milord, and so the people, who love her benign temper and humble wisdom without knowing her visions.

Eugenius: And you, our dear friend Bernard? You have kept silent. Tell us what you think—and why you gape so.

Bernard: Out of wonder rather than desire: these visions touch my soul.

Eugenius: As they do mine, Clairvaux. But you, Abbot, remain skeptical.

Kuno: Unconvinced, Milord. How does one prove visions, which may come from God or the Devil?

Eugenius: Can you believe such beauty and piety from the devil?

Kuno: Though she be sincere, she is simple, insistent, and, finally, Milord, but a woman.

Eugenius: And we, dear Abbot, are finally fearful, dust, and but men. The people do love this nun, and we would loath to see the Church, local or general, suffer from her censure when all can benefit from her talents and service. We do approve these remarkable visions, and with our thanks to all of you, we believe they may come from God and should be harbored, plenished, and praised as His gift. We declare this woman one of our living lights. Abbot, you will support and sustain our sister in her study, speech, and writing. For love of Christ do so.

Kuno: Holiness, shall we churchmen be led by a woman, and shall this woman drain the faith of the populace from us? We should wield God's pen and be God's flagons, filling souls with His spirit.

Herman: With His spirit or our own?

Eugenius: You must understand, Kuno, that we wish you no harm, but that we wish our Church good. As the Church flourishes, and as our flock flourish, so we flourish. Draw the water from the bread, and though it be but water, the flour blows away like dust. She tends the flowers that we may grow them, and she draws the hungry to us that we may feed them.

Kuno: And be fed by them. And to them. I defy this pragmatism, and I defy the vomit of these visions that reek of earth's decay rather than heaven. Have we no pride?

Eugenius: We too must wear our humility, Abbot, and take our bread from the servants God sends us. Now hear me: you will nurture our daughter Hildegard, the Flower of Prophecy, and through her we shall all be fed. I will not be forsworn. I tell you, support and encourage her and serve your Church.

Kuno: (Aside.) Mother Church.

Eugenius: Abbot?

Kuno: As you will, Holiness.

Eugenius: So we will. Come, my friends, let us rise and take some air. A cool wind blows at the window at last, I think, and our day has drawn long.

So they spoke. Kuno, you see, had no particular fondness for intellectual women. What had happened, he asked himself, since on one else was paying him any attention, to the proper order of things, to Degree, respect for Estates, as God the Father had built the world? As he must bear subservience to the Pope, so the woman should endure subservience to him. Who can trust, he thought, the visions of women, churned by emotion and tainted with the guilt of Eve? The pope could be right, of course, must be right, unless evil or, rather, weariness, or political currents had obscured his sight or maladjusted his thinking. Though he must encourage her work, though, he need not permit insubordination; in fact, Kuno appointed his own particular duty to keep the woman first on her course to salvation and only second on the paths of knowledge—rather, third, he thought, after also her devotion to the duty of obedience, a duty he as well as anyone might teach her, knowing its gall himself. The road home, long, difficult in any day, would give him room and time to brood, to meditate how best to direct her course and to restrain his disappointment.

Far away, back in Germania, among the Rupertsberg streets, a crowd gathered for a festival: a brief time of pleasure amidst lives hounded by pain and want. Three rustic travelers in bright costumes, such colors as few of the lower classes could legally wear in those times, danced acrobatically, strong eastern accents rolling the German obliquely off their tongues. They paused for applause, to gather themselves for the next performance, and to address their audience.

> Dayadva: Ai, those Russian crowds were tough. They like you, they stamp their feet, they don't like you, they stamp their feet: who knows what they think?
>
> Datta: At least they don't draw their swords. Remember Mongolia?
>
> Dayadva: Ai! How can I forget Mongolia?
>
> Damyata: At least they don't make borscht in Mongolia. Russia: borscht, borscht, borscht. Cold as a frozen schussbaba.
>
> Dayadva: Boy: watch your language.
>
> Datta: He's all right, Dayadva. He's coming of an age, and who can help but think of such things.
>
> Dayadva: That's all we need: Damyata girl chasing.
>
> Damyata: Yes, we definitely need that, yes.
>
> Datta: Both of you, calm yourselves. This crowd will be better than any people yet. I feel it. I know it.
>
> Dayadva: I hope you are right, old father. Perhaps we stay a while here before we move on to Italy.
>
> Damyata: They have nice girls in Italy?
>
> Datta: Nice brown-eyed girls. I remember.

Damyata: I like blue eyes.

Dayadva: First a frozen schussbaba, now he want to be picky about eye color.

Datta: Shhh, both. Dall comes. Let us prepare to do show.

When a crowed began to gather, having heard their instruments or having seen their dancing, the performers started to clap their hands and sing. The crowd, ever eager for carnival, or even the merest break from daily drudgery, gave the acrobats no gifts yet, but they did supply their attention, and that usually had a way of turning itself at least into supper for itinerant actors and their like. Hardly the abstract and brief chroniclers of their time, they often felt grateful for an edible meal and a bit of something sufficient to carry them to the next town. Overlooking the crowd, the eldest spoke first, shouting gleefully and rubbing his balding skull.

Datta: I am Datta, grandfather.

Dayadva: And I, Dayadva, father.

Damyata: And I, Damyata, son.

All three: And this is Dall, mother.

All four: We come from a far land: to entertain you!

They sang and danced to such musical accompaniment as simple instruments could provide: Donau, son of Dayadva's sister, simple of mind but devoted to his uncle, patted a tabor, turned a drone, or puffed into a shawm with more soul than talent or skill. Truly, they had invested nearly all of their wealth in their instruments and costumes, all but what they had spent on the horse and wagon that carried them from town to town.

In our poor, overfed age we may disdain such simple street-circus acrobatics as one could have found then, but the craftsfolk and peasants of Rupertsberg clapped along, sang or whistled with the performers when they knew the tunes, and gave at least a cheer, having little else to give and little else beyond work to do. Finding their song and dance had won praise, but nothing more material, and having learned something of the village before they performed, they enlisted help from members of their audience to perform a pantomime in which Dall, wife of Dayadva and mother of Damyata, costumed as a nun received a vision, was judged and nearly crucified by authorities, but was finally saved by a bright, mysterious figure dressed in blue. Her father-in-law, draped in a long, blue cloth, carrying before him a great mask in the shape of a smiling sun, strode before them, after which Dall moved among the crowed, healing her former persecutors and leading them all in a dance. Yes, folk would dance in those days, leaving their burdens for a few blessed moments beside the road until, reawakened by a soldier or official or priest, they would take them up once more. But on that day the sun and authorities alike shone, and even the bees seemed to stop in their course to observe and join the hum.

Datta: And now I, Datta, will perform a feat such as you have never seen before. Behold! And it is you who will save me from death.

He climbed upon a roadside wall, as his compatriots arranged and prepare some folk from the crowd to catch him. They well knew that if they won not only the admiration but the affection and familiarity of the people, they well might eat for the next several days, and regular meals make for strong and ready performers. Datta, making great show, spreading his arms wide, then straight overhead, sprung from his perch atop the wall into the human net his comrades had set for him; they caught him with a loud cheer not only for his courage, but for their own skill in breaking his fall. Datta sprung from their arms into a handspring, then bowed grandly.

> **Datta:** Such are the kind people here, to spare the life of an old man for another show. And such is the great lady of the abbey, that we dedicate our play to her, known far and wide for her kindness, gentleness, and holiness.

"Encore! Encore! Let's see it again, old Datta!" the crowd cried.

> **Dayadva:** No, Father, once a day is enough.

"Encore! Once more, Old Man!" they called again.

> **Datta:** They will have their show. Who are we to deny them? They buy our bread and milk—we hope.
>
> **Dayadva:** Care, Father, care!

Datta climbed again to the cheers of the crowd. They aligned themselves, but as well may happen in such instances, their attention wandered, and when Datta made his trusting dive, they failed to catch him, and he and they tumbled together to the ground.

> **Dayadva:** Father!
>
> **Crowd:** He is hurt! Help him!
>
> **Dayadva:** Father, why did I let you do it? What will we do?
>
> **Damyata:** The great lady on the hill, surely she will help him.
>
> **Dall:** Come, let us take him quickly to the abbess. She is a healer. Come, hurry! Help us, all of you!

The folk, sorry for their failure, but sorrier yet that they had got pulled into street acrobatics, dutifully lifted him and carried him up the hill to the nearby abbey to seek the help of the Great Lady on the Hill.

So their world brought them toward Hildegard's gate.

Above the town, at Disibodenberg Abbey in a long, bright hallway, the nuns sang the *Ordo Virtutum*, number 7, the "Song about the Virgins," a sober but joyful prayer, composed by Abbess Hildegard for their instruction and spiritual pleasure. The song drifted along like a breeze, as gentle to the singers as a waft of lilacs.

Irmengard: Lovely song.

Clementia: So long as we praise God and not ourselves.

Adelheid: So gloomy, Sister: can we not enjoy the song for the song?

Clementia: The song should guide us to God, not to ourselves and the dust of this world. Youth flies to pleasure rather than to Heaven.

Richardis: And may we not fly to both, joy in ourselves to be pleasures to God?

Clementia: Quite right, and wise for one so young. But let us not guide those younger yet astray.

Richardis: The devil flees such music; its coolness balms the soul and sends evil rushing from the flood of praise. So the song serves both God and us.

Adelheid: Thank you, Sister. I would learn and praise better.

Richardis: Then listen closely to Sister Clementia and heed her warnings; she will help you clear your path

> to heaven (Aside, to Adelheid she whispered then.)
> And be sure to enjoy the lovely songs!

As they paused from their singing to talk and enjoy the afternoon, Hildegard and Sister Keunegard joined them, walking arm-in-arm. Hildegard took great care with her charge, for the poor young woman, tall, thin, and pale, hung ever on the brink of madness.

> **Keunegard:** Praise, O praise, let us sing the song, the song, O cry whelps and mongrels at His coming, O cry dust and ashes, slave and king, blood and bone, tree and leaf.
>
> **Richardis:** How is she today, Mother Hildegard?
>
> **Hildegard:** God save her, not at her best. Yet even in her dark hours, she sings God's praise. Maybe we should all be so ill.
>
> **Keunegard:** O do sing, O pulchrace facies, O pulchace.

To please God and Keunegard, the nuns sang, and Sister Clementia guided them outside, leaving Hildegard and Sister Richardis alone to talk. Fast friends since the day the younger woman's wealthy family had placed her under Hildegard's instruction, they often sat or walked together in the garden to talk and solve the world's problems.

> **Nuns:** O pulchrace facies,
> Deum aspicientes et in aurora aedificantes,
> O beatae virgines, quam nobiles estis.

Hildegard and Richardis watched Keunegard as Clementia led her out.

> **Hildegard:** I believe she will be all right now that she is singing. She does love to sing. Please keep an eye on her, my dear. (Richardis followed Keunegard

and Clementia, and Hildegard worries aloud.) Poor Keunegard, she suffers so with doubt and longing, doubting what she hears, longing for confirming visions. Lord, I believe; help now my unbelief. How can we know the source of our visions, self or God? If self, even then they draw me to God, thus surely not Infernal. Finally, we know only God and dust. The rest is empty as air.

Richardis (returning, smiling): Keunegard seems fine now. We may leave her under Clementia's watchful eye, who would scare a lion into soft hymns.

Hildegard: I wish I knew what to do to help her. I do not want to discourage: her voices may come from God, and how well I know the silencing eye of authority and the choking muzzle of self-doubt.

Richardis: And yet you know your own visions, know them true. Do they not give some guide in hers?

Hildegard: I believe . . . I believe in my own visions because they burn upon my inner eye. How can I judge the burning of another's eye or the ringing in another's ear? Because I am an abbess, am I also a judge? I would open my heart to compassion and leave judgment to the Lord.

Richardis: But we must live holy and praise God, not defame Him among ourselves or others.

Hildegard: Maybe we praise by being. How can I silence another when I cannot silence myself, and would not? We must risk the voice of Satan to hear the voice of God. Prophecy weighs soul and body, circumscribes itself and pierces the heart—and damn the ill conse-

quence. An hour after, I may not know myself what I
have really seen, what may be God and what disease.

Richardis: Dearest Abbess and friend, you do know the
truth of your visions. I have seen you in their midst,
and I have seen them burn you, coming as they will,
at His will. Do you not feel them even now, for poor
Keunegard's sake? Can you offer her no respite from
ill dreams?

Hildegard: Perhaps I would deny mine for my sake even
as I would deny Keunegard's for hers. Believe me, they
burn. But you are right: a moment's memory turns
them noonday clear. Hotter to hold than a fire-tongs,
noisier than a dawn sky trumpeting spring rain they
come, and sometimes ease thereafter. I see them now.
The hand of God dips into my heart, and ever as the
eye pants after His glory, He speaks: "Know the ways
of the Lord; know His beauty." And the trembling
soul wakens with the beating of His voice to see the
earth give birth to the morning sun, for so His spirit
rises, a living fire, till my heart explodes in waves of
embers that flood the paling sky, take shape, and fall
again as God's joyous tears.

As Hildegard fell silent, allowing herself a moment's freedom to enter into the passions and sorrows of vision, footfalls pattered along the walkway, and Volmar, Hildegard's secretary, burst upon them breathless, his feet pattering rapidly on the stones.

Volmar: News from Rome, holy Abbess: the Pope has
graciously approved your work and would have you
complete it. God be praised! You should have seen his
face, lean and grave as a death mask, fit to grace a
cathedral door to admonish all to holiness, and Kuno,

of course, the old crab, scuttled about humphing and wishing for himself a cardinal's robe and red enough in the face to match it when the Pope himself praised and blessed your visions.

Hildegard: Dear Brother, please slow down and catch your breath. We have time to hear about Rome and your travels. But you look thin. Are you well?

Volmar: Thin from joy and pale from awe at the holy city, a city such as you have never seen, Sister, splendid, bright with gold, churning with pomp: who could eat in such a place? And the caravans of pilgrims, constant as the rush and flood of the Tiber!

Hildegard: Then praise be to God you are free again of gold and pomp, and we have pilgrims enough here among the poor and sick who need our care.

Volmar: You are a little Rome in yourself, Sister. You open eyes with faith and hearts with love, seal wounds with weeds, sooth harms with herbs, and move the slack soul with music. My pilgrimage was not there, but here, to serve God by serving you.

Hildegard: Serve God, not me, and we will all win His praise. Welcome home, my friend. Has the Abbot arrived also?

Volmar: Yes, and I have no doubt you shall see him soon.

Hildegard: Well, be that as it must. Brother, I have more to dictate soon and letters to write. Please come tomorrow.

Volmar: At your pleasure, Abbess. Oh, Abbess, one more thing. How can I say this? We should arrange for secretarial duty for you when I am gone.

Hildegard: Richardis serves me in your absence and can do so again when you travel.

Volmar: I thought to make provision for after my death, Abbess.

Hildegard: Surely we need not. You will outlive me. You had better, Brother.

Volmar: The work is too important to take a chance that no one will be here to replace me.

Hildegard: Let us not talk of that now. Life goes as it will, and God has given me you and Richardis as help and friends. For now let us attend to the present and its visions.

Volmar: Yes, Abbess.

The dutiful secretary bowed to both women and left them. Richardis' blue eyes shone, and her smile showed healthy white teeth unusual in those days of the world.

Richardis: Voluble he is as the creeks when the snow melts in spring, and flitting as a sparrow.

Hildegard: But kind and chaste, faithful and good.

The two women heard a rustle of voices and many feet coming up the pathway. The nuns led the folk of the town, who carried Datta, injured in his fall, and brought him before the abbess.

Hildegard: How can we help you?

Dayadva: Dear Lady, poor Father is hurt from a fall performing in the marketplace. Please help him. He is our life and living. We have heard you can heal. Help him, please.

Hildegard: (She looks at him, then speaks to Richardis.) Boil water and bring cloth and ashes of blackthorn, also apple salve. Take Irmengard to assist you. Clementia, clear some space for us here. Adelheid, prepare a bed of soft rushes in the infirmary. (To Datta:) How are you? Can you speak?

Datta: Foolish, as old men often are.

Dayadva: He took a fall upon his head. I fear the arm and shoulder broke, too.

Dall: Do help him, Lady. Dear old father.

Hildegard: I'll do all I can. God willing, we shall find healing for him, or at least some ease for his pain. Let us try the arm. A slight pull here. Yes. (He yells. Irmengard enters with cloths and bandages. Hildegard takes one of the cloths and binds and slings his arm and shoulder. Richardis enters with a pot of water and medicines.) Here, apply a poultice of the blackthorn to his head after you clean the wound. I will use the salve on his face and eyes. How are you, Old Father?

Datta: I think the world will put up with me somedeal longer.

Hearing that, the crowd cheered, partly for the old acrobat's well-being, partly out of relief that their day need meet no further interruption, and partly because they wondered and feared if the mere presence of the famous Abbess had not been sufficient to heal him. Young Datta glanced from Hildegard's eyes to his grandfather's wounds to the luminous young face of Adelheid.

Hildegard: Take him to the infirmarr—gently! He will need rest, but I believe he will be all right. We will pray for him.

Dall: Thank you, Lady.

Datta: We cannot thank enough. We must pay.

Hildegard: Don't worry about pay. Care for your father and pray. And caution him about such stunts in the future.

Datta: Who can tell old man what to do?

Dall: Da, who can?

Damyata: Bless you, Lady. Will you help the great Lady, young woman?

Adelheid: I will do what I can to assist, of course.

Damyata: Then I believe Grandfather shall live.

The folk, guided by Hildegard's nuns, carried Datta to the infirmary, cheerfully singing a drinking song as they went, not thinking so much about where they found themselves as feeling a glee that a fellow creature had, they believed, had cheated death. Hildegard waited to take a breath of air and calm her mind of visions.

Having fallen in together at the end of the train of folk, Adelheid and Damyata briefly caught each other's eyes. They paused, blushed. Each stammered a word, then the two hurried to catch up with the others. Their feet fell so lightly, propelled with the energy of youth, that they almost seemed to Hildegard to skip. When the watchful nun was free of migraines, little escaped her attention.

Hildegard: This injury we can heal, but what about the next? Who knows? How close we are to love, and how close to death.

In those days monks and nuns often shared abbeys, though they lived largely segregated lives. At the opposite end of Disibodenberg Abbey lived a cadre of monks. They entered the abbey through the main public hall that connected, through heavy, locked doors, the halves of the community. Shying away from the ruckus opposite, they prepared to welcome their abbot, Kuno, who had just returned from the synod in Rome.

First monk: Word is she has had the work approved by the Pope himself.

Second monk: And that she has had a vision proclaiming she should move her nuns to Rupertsberg.

First monk: We know what the abbot will say to that. She brings money to the abbey from the rich and powerful. Alms come from everywhere for her prayers, and gifts have arrived the last three days as thanks for her healings. Everyone knows her, from peasants to kings.

Third monk: Better say nothing to the abbot. I would not even whisper. He returned from Rome smoking like the very devil.

Second monk: I am sure by now he has heard about the move.

First monk: He will not approve it.

Third monk: That does not matter. She is a friend of Rome and now, according to Rome, a prophet.

First monk: Imagine that! Now wee shall see some sparks fly between heaven and hell.

Third monk: Quiet.

Abbot Kuno had entered more quietly than a breeze. His face showed no particular expression at all beyond his usual military self-control.

Kuno: Singing lauds, Lads?

Monks: Lauds, Abbot?

Kuno: What I heard sounded more like whispers than vespers.

First Monk: In humor, Abbot?

Kuno: Rather, out of humor: the choler galls me. This sister galls me. Perhaps I had better let her move.

Second Monk: It is true, then.

Kuno: Yes, if that will stop your tittering.

Third Monk: And shall the move be approved?

Kuno: You know as well as I how dependent we are upon her—how shall I say it—attractiveness to the people.

Third Monk: Kings, queens, even Popes . . .

Kuno: Your sincerity does not escape us. She shall not move short of papal approval. Now give up your clucking and sing, hens. God waits for no man, no, nor for woman, either. Now go, and sing a *Requiem*.

Third Monk: For whom, Milord?

Kuno: For you, if you do not do as I say.

The Monks hurriedly left him, singing their requiem, as their lord required. What choice had they?

Monks: Requiem aeternam, dona eis domine; Et lux perpetua, Luceat eis.

Such chants often filled the monks' time until the next Canonical Hour, as the rich would pay abbeys to sing prayers for their own souls as well as for those of their children and friends, often to perpetuity. The abbot began fiddling with a jumbled collection of rolled folio-style pages, refocusing his thoughts.

> **Kuno: Right: perpetual light. Oh, I am weary of the long years. Perhaps *the woman* could heal me. I will tend to my letters till she comes. Letters, letters, letters. Sheepskin for the sheeps' souls' sake, perhaps. God save us and bring us all our souls' medicine.**

As silently as Kuno had crept up to his monks, Hildegard approached her abbot, who stood lost in his thoughts. She composed herself. When her thoughts were free of vision and her body free of pain, her long, kind face shone with a natural gentility buoyed with openness and pleasure in human exchange that a man such as Kuno easily mistakes for simpering pride. Hildegard knew from experience that Kuno hated that look, so she did her best to compose her facial muscles to bland silence.

> **Hildegard: God heals whom He will—sorry if I startled you, Abbot. I merely follow the instructions He gives and depend upon the faith of patient and physician alike. Sometimes I fear the cure above the disease, as though I sew an herbal tapestry only to smother my patient in his own pain and hang his life upon a thread. I must weave mosaics of my faith, for God and in me. If I do not, where can the Suffering turn? To God, yes, but in this world, to ease their pain, to me or nowhere. God bless you, Father Abbot, and welcome home.**

> **Kuno: You. Your writing has been approved by the synod; the Pope himself proclaims you prophetess. For his sake, mine, and yours, I urge you take approval hum-**

> bly and gratefully and pursue this course carefully. This human dust pares whiskers when it seeks alone to discriminate the voice of God and the wiles of Satan. Be patient and loath to speak without certainty. Evil counsel and false vision lead the gullible astray and demean the Church in men's eyes, and the reputation of the Church must remain inviolate. And by the way, I must turn down your request to move your nuns' quarters to Rupertsberg. You need priestly guidance and protection, especially since the masses who come to seek prayer and healing seem to grow daily. Nuns depend upon their priests and brothers; so it has been and shall be. Since you were tithed to us at eight years of age, you have been willful, and willfulness comes not from God. We will hear no more of this matter. Good day, Sister.

With no further pleasantries, he left.

> Hildegard: Has the abbot ears? I know he has eyes to seek me out and tongue to chastise. I gather he can tell a rose from a chamber pot. And I have heard he eats his bread and cheese with none the less relish for his being an abbot. I wish he too would have a vision, so that he could understand it means responsibility and doubt, not seeking after personal glory.

Then Hildegard felt a vision rising before her. From a misty figure in the growing afternoon shadows she heard the voice of Jutta, her mentor and friend, the abbess who had raised her from childhood and brought her to the land of learning and spirituality.

Spirit of Jutta: Be quick to trust and respect your abbot. Be wary of trust and pride in words, and question what you see.

Hildegard: Though you yourself are only a vision, dear Jutta, teacher and friend. You who raised me, died and left me abbess, have you no more to tell me?

Spirit: Hear also: what have you but works and visions? The are the truest part of you. The rest is mere illusion.

Hildegard: Either way, substanceless. She speaks as if I want these visions. Oh, I am tired. The sick I can manage, but these visions bend me toward the grave.

Richardis found Hildegard there as the vision dispersed again into shadows. She propped up her mentor with a strong, young shoulder.

Richardis: May I impose upon your thoughts?

Hildegard: No imposition to turn my thoughts to God or you.

Richardis: You are perhaps too hard on the abbot and do not spare him for his inherited choler.

Hildegard: If he were melancholy, I could cure him: dip him twice by the hair in cold, white water. The idea appeals to me anyway, I must admit. But only kindness kills choler, and he will have none of it, though he put this nun to the perpetual rack. But come sit by me and tell me what you are thinking.

Richardis: I came to console, since I heard the abbot close the door to Rupertsberg.

> **Hildegard:** Eavesdropping is a sin, my child, and why listen to the fall of a rusty gate when you could be listening to the birds at the window?
>
> **Richardis:** Because I would protect and defend my second mother. If only we were taught like the wrestlers at the festival in the marketplace. I should tie the abbot in a circle, lead him by the arm to the gate of Rupertsberg, and bid him bless it.
>
> **Hildegard:** Peace, Child, God bids us peace, though I could stand to see that wrestling hold myself. But just now I feel the fragrance of the lilac through the window and would dress the wounds of the poor old man before compline and the fall of the bread beneath the cunning bats falls...
>
> **Richardis:** Dear Mother, you grow pale. Are you faint?
>
> **Hildegard:** No, no, God holds us up even as the gate crumbles at our feet...
>
> Hildegard fainted at Richardis' feet.
>
> **Richardis:** Clementia, come quick! The abbess! Help me!

Back among the Rupertsberg streets, through a broad, common square, monks walked in prayerful peripiteia, singing their requiem, "Requiem aeternam, dona eis Domine . . ." as a crowd of people, half in awe, half incredulously, watched and listened to them. The acrobatic clowns fell in line behind them, mimicking. The monks, ignoring them, walked along in their prayers. Soldiers, seeing the fun and wondering if they should laugh or subdue the actors, came up the road from the opposite way, marching and maneuvering to martial drums. Once again the clowns fell in line, but behind the soldiers, mimicking them comically, to the restrained delight of the crowd. The soldiers paused, eyeing the clowns, then pursued their own way, satisfied that they carried their dignity with them. Then to slow, dirge-like drums a bedraggled array of pilgrims, one carrying a cross, others moaning and groaning in time with the drums, entered the square from a side street. Some flagellated themselves, and some just hobbled along, crying woefully or sweating in silence. The crowd remained, staring at this new vision of humanity that bestowed itself upon them. The clowns peered closely at the pilgrims, shrugged to themselves, and departed in dismay: even their humor had its boundaries. Such street scenes enlivened the town as the sun traced its decent to nightly death, leaving earth's creatures, weary and hungry, to fend off her darkness as best they could.

Back at the Abbey the infirmary remained busy through the night and into the morning with its mismatch of patients. The nuns traded watch, and before the dew rose from the grass, Sister Clementia entered to take her shift watching them.

Richardis: Thank you for coming for me, Sister. I sat with her all night. What do you think?

Clementia: She does poorly. She is drenched with fever. I have spent the night preparing medicines such as the Abbess has in the past instructed me.

Richardis: Most of the night she talked out of her head.

Clementia: You may rest if you wish. Irmengard and Adelheid will come shortly. How does the acrobat?

Richardis: He recovers nicely, believe it or not. Please keep a close eye. I fear for Hildegard.

The two woman stood over their friend and mentor. Richardis spoke softly to the sleeping woman.

Richardis: Once again they drive you to the abyss with their doubting. I believe in you, dear second mother, and will stay by you to wipe your burning brow.

Hildegard: Darkness, darkness, and the burning. Will they not stop the burning? The eyes are burning, the mouth, the ears, the nose, burning.

As Hildegard rambled, the poor, mad Keunegard entered wringing her hands, her eyes rolling.

Hildegard: All that touches them burns.

Keunegard: Yes, yes, my dear, they burn us, they burn, I hear them now, coming with their knives and torches, their sharp, hollow harps and torches. Keep them from us, keep them from us, Oh God, keep them from us.

Sisters Irmengard and Adelheid entered the infirmary to share the morning watch. Richardis addressed Sister Irmengard.

Richardis: Please take Sister Keunegard outside. She must not disturb the abbess. She is gravely ill.

Keunegard: I must not leave her! She needs me to protect her. They flame and spout. They are coming; they are coming!

Clementia led the young nun from the sickroom, Adelheid following.

Hildegard: Tormentil and tansy. Tormentil and tansy, mixed with honey. The darkness and the burning. Tormentil and tansy.

Irmengard: Do you understand what she wants?

Richardis: Yes, I believe so. She is not entirely out of her head, I think. Please bring tormentil, dornella, that is, the root, and tansy leaves mixed in honey and wine. You'll find them both on the herb shelf. How is Keunegard?

Adelheid (who has re-entered as Irmengard exits): Clementia has calmed her and taken her for a walk.

Richardis: Poor Clementia: she has so many duties here she will wear herself out.

Adelheid: She is tough as stones. We all know it.

Richardis: But even she must rest. I think someone should call the abbot. If the drugs she has called for from her dream will not work, I fear we will lose her. Have we heard from the Archbishop of Mainz?

Adelheid: I do not know. I do know the abbot will be angry.

Richardis: Then let his anger weigh him like a stone and drown him. This fever has lasted too long.

Irmengard (returning): Here is the drug. I have warmed the wine a bit.

Richardis: You are an angel. Let us hope it suffices.

Richardis did her best to get Hildegard to drink from the cup. The abbess sipped, then coughed.

Hildegard: Rupertsberg, Rupertsberg. The word of the Lord. The tongue is burning, burning.

Richardis: Try to drink a bit more, Mother. We hope we have made the medicines as well as you so often have taught us. . . .

In the Abbot's quarters Kuno paced and brooded. A monk entered carrying a message printed on an old sheet of vellum.

Monk: The letter from the Archbishop of Mainz, Milord.

Kuno: Do not bother to read it. I know what it says: same as the letters from Bishop Herman and Bishop Hartwig. It seems this woman will have her way. How she galls me, like a fire in my belly or a vulture gnawing at my liver. Perhaps I must be rid of her. You may go. (Kuno continues, alone, to himself.) Prophet, prophetess. What prophets gain a man the world only to take it from him with his own soul? The spume and spray of prophecy, vulgar as the breaking and spitting of a penniless pilgrim's pack horse, who can believe in it? This woman who gets her wish or takes to her deathbed, sending half of Christendom packing letters off to the Pope for her safety and succor, what has she done to deserve this grace of God, if it be from God, to hear the Master's voice, see his visions and speak them through her own lips? I saw her myself crawl upon her knees at tender years, not above eight, her parents' tithe to God and the abbey, and then her eyes looked common enough. And now she has drawn the attention of all the world, and all the Christian world speaks her name with reverence, and I, who have said "Yes, Your Holiness," and touched his hand, lack the first notes of a heavenly voice and the first flickers of a vision. And she has got the best of me. Whether she have a soul or not, she has gamed with me like boys marbling in the streets and taken me for the treasure of my own soul. Let her go and let her live, then, or let her die, if that may be God's will. And then my abbey will become her shrine and sepulchre and so a hundred generations of Kunos will be bound as prey to her. I will drive her from me like a frothing dog.

The monk reluctantly re-entered his abbot's room and thoughts.

Monk: The nuns are calling for you, Milord. The abbess falls near death.

Kuno: Only near? I come. Slowly, slowly as soldiers do on parade, with dignity, and perhaps I shall be too late.

At the Infirmary the nuns kept close watch on their beloved Hildegard. As Richardis spoke to them, Abbot Kuno entered with some reluctance. He felt his brow knotting and did his best to quiet it.

Richardis: She has taken double doses of the medicine and still burns hot as iron in the noonday sun. She is as she was before she began to dictate her visions, when ignorant of God's intent she kept His word to herself, afraid of blasphemy or calling undue attention to herself. And now this humblest of gifted creatures nears her death for want of an abbot's mercy. May his dust burn with the fever of her visions.

Kuno: The dust himself is here and brings pardon. You have stayed too long with your willful abbess and have learned her pride and have filed a sharp tongue of your own. Despite my fears for you, your mistress, and your sisters, I must spring this lot of plundering sparrows to their own nest. Word comes from the archbishop that you shall have your abbey. You may prepare your move to Rupertsberg. But I doubt your abbess shall join you there. How is she? The room smells of camphor.

Richardis: Blessed news, perhaps too late: the fever will not leave her. It may yet relent, though without her guidance we pray and guess about the medicines.

Kuno: Willfulness wins the day, but obedience wins heaven. I would see her better, but the air is close here.

Richardis: Better not to come too close: she needs her air and may be contagious.

Clementia: And she certainly needs to rest without the intrusion of men and their prying. Back to your duties and leave us to ours.

Kuno: This pride seems a fault of all the sex, though frailty be the flaw of only one.

He left the nuns to their work.

Richardis: If only you could hear, dear Mother, perhaps the news that you may now perform God's will would give you peace. Do you know me? Do you know the devoted one who attends you? Think of the visions you have told me and from whom they come, the countless stars dropping from the heavens in the ancient night, the cosmic tree that radiates from God, delves with its limbs and its roots and spreads its leaves into the divine mystery, Mother Wisdom who fishes for souls and dries them in the robes of the church, the golden spirit of poverty, chastity, and service sweeping upon the humble and elect. Oh, hear me, Mother.

Hildegard: Daughter, I hear you. Are you too having visions? I feel as though I am rising from a dead sleep. I dreamed that the abbot was here.

Richardis: Mother, Mother, do not speak too much. You are weak, but I feel the fever breaking from you even now. The August northerly drives the stale air off the vineyard to let the ripe grapes breathe just so: remember it.

Hildegard: The abbot?

Richardis: The Archbishop has approved our move. The abbot has freed us.

Hildegard: With a cry from his own pockets, no doubt.

Richardis: Rest now, true Abbess, abbess of your own convent, to be built on the hill in Rupertsberg, overlooking the river.

Hildegard: Again I may believe that God directs me. Dear, do you have anything to wet my throat?

Richardis: You called for tormentil and tansy in wine.

Hildegard: Maybe a sip more, to wash the torment from this tangent and transient life. Even a sip of water will do.

A few days later, in the Rupertsberg streets, the folk crowded the main square as the acrobats performed their act, creating in tandem and allegorical pantomime. As they danced, Keunegard watched them from the hill just above. Datta, still wearing his sling, and Dayadva, taking the role of mock-priests, danced, then when Dall joined the dance, they, mugging at the crowd, carried Dall to a cross as if to crucify her. Damyata appeared, dressed in a simple robe, from amidst the crowd to drive the two "priests" away, release Dall, and lead her before the crowd, where they danced together. Datta and Dayadva returned, dressed as the dirty pilgrims who the day before had migrated through the square, moaning and groaning, one flogging himself and the other carrying a small cross. Dall and Damyata watched them, shook their heads sadly and exaggeratedly, then disappeared among the crowd as the other two hid behind a screen to change costumes. All four returned, dressed as simple peasants to conclude with an elaborate dance, accompanied by the slow beat of Donau's drum. As they danced, to the mixed delight and disgust of the crowd the dirty pilgrims returned and slowly crossed the makeshift stage of the city street, moaning and flagellating themselves. A pilgrim carrying a large cross passed among the crowd, stumbled and fell. Dayadva bent to help him rise, but the pilgrim pushed him away, stumbled again, and barely managed to lift his cross and stagger after the retreating pilgrims. Dayadva sadly returned to his comrades.

Dayadva: We try.

Datta: We try.

Dall: The people look sad now. Shall we do show again?

Datta: Let us do show again.

Dayadva: We do show . . . maybe not. Not I am feeling so good sudden.

Dall: What is wrong?

Dayadva: Head begins to spin. Ah, will be fine. We do show again.

With the departure of the pilgrims, the people began to fill the square, milling uncomfortably, but events moved rapidly once again from drama to trauma. A poor girl, Sigewize by name, emerged from amidst the crowd. She was dressed in torn, floppy men's garments. The acrobats began again to dance, but stopped as Sigewize, tearing at her hair, began to scream horrifically, rushing among them, flinging her arms wildly.

Sigewize: Lucifer! Beelzebub! Moloch and Mammon! Drink the blood and fry the salmon! Toads, you're

all toads burning in the sun, frying to ashes. Where's my knife? I'll cut you. Run, damned Vipers, run, Abominations, Stillborns, Dung, Demons. Drink your own blood. You'll get none of mine. O you, O you, faceless ones from the stinking pits, I'll cut you!

Hearing the girl scream, Keunegard from above held out her arms and called to her.

Keunegard: Oh Sister, Sister! God has sent you to me. Do not let them hurt you. I come; I come!

Sigewize screamed again, snarled, and pulling a knife from her cloak, swung it at a butcher who until then had paid her little attention. Several men in the crowd caught and restrained her, took her knife, and held her down, trying to figure out what to do with her as the poor girl screamed madly. Keunegard, seeing the struggle, rushed down the pathway to the street and threw herself down beside the girl.

Keunegard: Peace, peace, I know God has sent you to me to be healed. You shall drink of my blood and be healed, and God will have you for his heaven.

If the townsmen had felt confused before, this double dose of madness paralyzed them, and Sigewize broke free and struck Keunegard to the ground. Once again the crowd restrained her as she screamed and writhed, but too late to save the young nun from injury.

"Tie her! Kill her! No, hold her tight and take her to the abbess," called various folk. "The abbess! Yes, to the abbess!" Several together carried the girl Sigewize, while others took up the burden of the injured Keunegard. The first group made their way up the hill to the abbey, hoping that the wise lady could help, fearing that the very devil had found his way into their midst; the second group, the acrobats among them, paused, assessing the nun's condition.

Datta: I think the nun badly hurt.

Dall: Hurt, but not badly. I think we take her too to the abbess.

Dayadva: And take me, too. I fear I faint.

His skin turned milky white. His eyes open but empty, Dayadva collapsed at their feet.

"Father! Help!" they cried to a crowd whose sympathies and attention were already overspent.

As Dall held her husband's head in her hands, Damyata dashed among the markets, begging the merchants for someone to help them carry his stricken father to the hospital of the magical abbess.

Chapter Two

In the abbey above the town, monks and nuns in their separate cloisters chanted the hours in smooth plainsong. In the town below as they labored people sang saints' praises if they knew them, spells and charms if they thought no one was listening, or ballads of ghosts and heroes or simple, rousing drinking songs, especially when they had the time and means to stop for food.

On any given Wednesday the cloistered community tended the sick or their gardens, keeping the rooms and halls spartan and spotless, studied their few books in Latin, packed lightly for journeys to preach or collect alms or tend the varied flocks of the hamlets, prepared food or mended clothing or tools for themselves or the poorest townsfolk. The townsfolk practiced their crafts, performed or sloughed off their labors, built or mended boats for the river, tended their children, argued with their neighbors, attended masses when they might, washed their faces for weddings and funerals, and conducted the business of living as well as they could do.

In the library at Disibodenberg Abbey, Hildegard and Volmar spoke together of things past, passing, and to come. He would often write as she spoke, interjecting a question or a "hmm" or nodding assent to show that he had heard or to slow her down so he might copy accurately. They worked well together, and through practice their thoughts had come to follow predictable patterns.

Volmar: You begin the move tomorrow?

Hildegard: We have already started, moving necessities, furniture, and medicines. The building will take work, but we can at least move in. All work is God's work, if we do it in His praise.

Volmar: And what of your visions? Have they slowed from the illness and all the work?

Hildegard: Were I not wishing against God, I would wish them away, but they come hungry and fast as flies in spring. They buzz, they whirl, they bite. I can hardly shut them out long enough to say prayers and do my duties. Duties aplenty at that: we have had to call soldiers of the king to keep out pilgrims for a few days, or we would all go mad with the rush. Yes, my friend, the visions come. Even now, as I pause a moment, they swell into view. I see the mystical body of the living light taming a mad worm, foul and abysmal, spewing shafts of poison from its corrupt lips and body, wrapped in black flame. This gangrene brings decay and death, this Satan, but even as it spews forth its horrors, chained in the burning pits, a golden fire falls from the white-robed host of heaven to trample the beast. Its poison can't touch them. And I see the blue-robed virtues building the House of Wisdom, all colors they are, from the corners of the earth and heavens building a palace of souls in the palm of the Creator's hand. Past them all flies the flame-red head of Jehovah, spread-winged, righteous, guardian of women and children, of the sick and poor and oppressed, gathering the just at the center of the universe to form the living stones of the eternal temple of God.

Volmar: Praise God in earth and heaven. You draw the breath from me, turn me to a bleating lamb crying after the milk of the Lord.

Hildegard: So are we all, so should we all, as we lap the milk of His visions. Do we not all have visions when He calls us all to His living temple? Oh to pass from the frozen, lightless world, to be a stone beneath His feet in the eternal church where all instants and all atoms praise Father and Mother God in simultaneous eternity, drawn in the circle of the living light and pierced by the hand of divine love.

Volmar: Amen and amen. And what do you hear? Tell me the song they sing, that we sing—may we sing it with them? Ach! What is that noise? It sounds like a hundred devils.

In a great whirlwind of noise, Clementia, her broad feet slapping on the floor, burst in, interrupting their recording session. Like Hildegard, Clementia had an air of authority, her step and back firm, her brown eyes burning with intensity.

Clementia: The crowd, Abbess—even I cannot stop them. They bring a young woman possessed by demons. She raves like the pit itself. Keunegard has been hurt, too, but I believe she is all right.

Hildegard: Let them come. Please attend to Keunegard; I will see her as soon as I can. And bring the others, and send for the abbot. We must do an exorcism. But send Richardis first for drugs: cold wine, emerald shards, sprays of the fir and spruce, and old bread with the mold just beginning to grow on it.

The nuns and the monk hurried to the abbey's common hall. A crowd of townsfolk had arrived with Sigewize, the mad girl, bound and gagged. She lay on the floor staring, moaning, and writhing painfully, trying to bite through the dirty gag with which they had bound her mouth. Without their conviction that Hildegard would know what to do with her, they may well have killed her or allowed her to kill herself.

> **Hildegard:** Must you bind her so? She is a human being, not an animal.
>
> **1st Man:** Sorry, Milady. We tried to keep her from biting and scratching us, and she was shouting things would make the devil blush.
>
> **Hildegard:** Then take her to the infirmary, and when the nuns and priests come, God shall save her. Do at least remove that gag, Clementia.
>
> **Sigewize:** Burn, Hell-witch. Lucifer strip you in black flame. Unbind me, O I will cut you and drink your blood.
>
> **1st Man:** Come, lads, these ladies should not hear such talk. Makes my hairs stand on end. May we carry her to the infirmary? Let's go, men.

As soon as the crowd had cleared, Dall came forward tentatively to speak to Hildegard. As she did, her family, aided by a few of the townsfolk, carried in Dayadva on a makeshift litter. As she spoke, Sister Adelheid entered from a side hallway. Before she could stop herself, she had caught Damyata's eye. Holding his glance a bit too long, she blushed, and so did he.

> **Dall:** Milady, pardon. My husband, he is sick, sick. Please help him. He helped one of the mad pilgrims, and we

do our show to make the people happy again, and he falls in the street. God help him! What I shall do?

Hildegard: I will look at him.

Adelheid: You are needed in the infirmary, Abbess.

Hildegard: I am needed here. They can begin there without me. While you wait for the priests, have Irmengard place emerald upon her breast, fir sprigs around her face, burn the spruce for its aroma, and get her to drink as much cold wine as she can.

Adelheid: Irmengard?

Hildegard: No, the young woman. Hurry. You, madam, must serve your husband, you your son, and you your father, while I get medicines. I fear he holds on by a nail's breadth. May health or eternal ease come upon him quickly. His forehead burns, and his eyes glaze. Can you hear me, good Man? Attend him. I will hurry.

Volmar: I am here, should you need me.

Hildegard: As ever you are, Brother.

In the Rupertsberg streets monks trod their usual path singing their usual *Requiem* after the fashion they so often followed, fulfilling their duty to the rich families who had paid to have relatives' souls sung perpetually. The usual dirty pilgrims entered the town square from the opposite way, groaning and crying, their drum beating out the rhythm of their ponderous pilgrimage. Various mad folk milled about the crowd, moaning and making faces at the folk who kept their stands of vegetables and dried and salted meats. One of the pilgrims began suddenly to turn cartwheels, kicking up great whirling clouds of dust. Behind them, at a safe distance from the dust, came a man robed and hooded like a monk, walking alone. When he reached the square, he stopped a workman who was passing, carrying his tools on the way to the local wheelwright's shed. He drew back his hood, uncovering a round, slightly doughy face, different than one would expect of a man whose feet were worn with travels. His large eyes with their completely round whites gave the impression that he concentrated fully upon the person with whom he was speaking and listened with a perpetual astonishment. He stopped and spoke first to himself and then to a roadside laborer who stood briefly to watch the pilgrims pass.

> Bernard: I come from Clairvaux to see the prophetess, and I find nothing but madness. God knows they need her here. In appearance ordinary, in mind and manner extraordinary, they say of her. Her words and visions I have read, and in them meet the godliest mind of our time. I would pray with her and of her as well as for her. That must be the abbey, on the hill above the river. A lovely, place, where ermine and fox play by the river and everything smells of pine, such a place where one could shake off the dust of old devotion for the joy of fresh prayer. Will I find Abbess Hildegard at this convent?
>
> 2nd Man: Surely, Father, I don't know.
>
> Bernard: You work so near and do not know who serves as abbess?
>
> 2nd Man: Surely St. Hildegard is abbess there.
>
> Bernard: You just told me that you did not know who is abbess.
>
> 2nd Man: I said I didn't know if you would find her there. She may be out, or you may not be able to find her.

Bernard: Be sure, I am able. But you should not call her saint, since she yet lives.

2nd Man: Many a saint should be as saintly as she, you and me included, and few better deserve the name.

Bernard: I believe you speak truly. To the abbey.

Guided by the laborer Bernard pressed on, while at the abbey Hildegard and her colleagues, who had sought to still the spirit of the afflicted young woman, took a welcome break from their work.

Priest: That was not easy. She writhed like a serpent and vomited fire. I believe she was possessed by Satan himself.

Monk: I have seen nothing short of war so terrifying as her twistings and mawings.

Priest: I cannot be certain she is well. I think you will have trouble with her yet.

Hildegard: We will continue prayers and masses for her and will feed her brine herring and cool wine. If I have not packed it, I have some sparrowhawk ointment to rub on her face and belly; that should cool the fever. And we will test her with a shard of topaz to see if the poison of the demon has left her.

Priest: God bless all, and luck be with you. You will need it. I must have some rest and food. You will, I trust, excuse me.

Hildegard: I will trust that God be with me, I think, and thank you for your labors, Father.

As she sat on a bench for a breath, Hildegard saw young Sister Adelheid approaching lithely, her face fixed and grave. The acrobats plodded sadly behind her.

> **Adelheid:** Abbess, I am sorry to tell you: Dayadava, the acrobat from the town, has gone to God. His poor family . . .
>
> **Hildegard:** The horned beetle survives the frost, the brown bear avoids the hunter's snare, the eel slithers from the angler's hook, but not one good man survives once death has cast on him his hungry eye. We must believe it for the best and long for the day when we shall see flesh revived, when all join in the one family of God. Though we know so, we never suffer loss easily.

Datta, Dall, Damyata, having left Donau with the townsfolk, knelt sorrowfully before the great lady.

> **Datta:** I believed you could save him. It come so quick, no time to ready, to say good-bye.
>
> **Hildegard:** I believed so, too, and I grieve with you; he was youthful and strong. We are but dust and fill this hourglass betimes, till time shake us loose and scatter this sullied flesh over the earth, that our souls may seek heaven. Bound by life, we are pierced by death, and whether the angel brings love, vision, honor, grace, fall, she brings mortality as well. God save you.
>
> **Dall:** We believe you did your able, and pray God save you, Lady.
>
> **Damyata:** What shall we do without Father? We are now a body without a soul.

Hildegard: You must do what you have always done. God has made you as you are to bring solace to the people of the towns, and you must do no less than His will. You have been called and chosen, and now your father watches from heaven. Would you disappoint him—or God?

Dall: Sure not, Lady. Come, Damyata, and Father Datta. We will grieve and then return to the market to dance. God be with you, Lady.

Hildegard: And also with you.

Damyata: (To Adelheid:) God be with you, young miss.

Adelheid: And with you, young man. Please be careful. We will pray for you. You must remain well to care for your family.

Damyata: I shall, for I take your blessing with me. You must come see us dance.

Adelheid: My work lies here at the abbey. But I will try. Come, friends. I will take you where you can make arrangements and get some rest.

Hildegard sat alone as clouds obscured the sun, the grey sky fitting her dulled spirits. She thought aloud, partly pondering, partly praying, the fingers of her right hand drumming rhythmically on her left arm.

Hildegard: Hard to give comfort when I find none or hope when I wonder what to hope for. How will they live now? Why can I heal one, when another's cure lies distant from me as the stars? These pilgrims bring plague, suffering, and death. Can we cast a devil from this child, if a devil it be that plagues her? Can I care for my nuns at Rupertsberg and keep them on the path to God? And can I learn to rejoice in these visions, if visions from God they be? Visions, yes, and from God, where else? How can I still doubt? So often they crest and toss distant as some ship shrouded in the grey mist. If the soul were a sea, I could sound its depths. However wide, however changing, rough as pummice or smooth as Leviathan's belly, I could bring the truth bobbing to the top, pierce its skin, bleed it clean. In dreams I fly, press my lips to the feet of God. My medicines sit tangible in my palms: herbs, decoctions, stones; prayer incarnates at the lips and the tongue, but visions tear away like a lost soul. But oh, when they come, they burn into the backs of my eyes and dance upon my brain. Young woman: out of your bed so soon? You must rest. You have suffered body and soul.

Sigewize had crept in as Hildegard sat with her thoughts. Spotting the girl, she had spoken gently to her. The girl replied, half restraining herself, unsure of how to respond to Hildegard's gentle and assured manner, the likes of which she had seen little in her short life.

Sigewize: Belial, is't you? Stay back! I will strike you. They have taken my knife, or I would cut the breasts from you that you could suckle no more demons. Is that you, Mother? Protect me from the priests and soldiers, Mother. I will not go down to the lake again, though the apples and cherries are blooming. You aren't my mother. Who are you?

Hildegard: I am Hildegard, abbess here, and here I will protect you, and God will protect you. Be at ease, Child.

Sigewize: At ease, at ease. Will they come for me and take me away, with their burning eyes and flaming tongues and their charred hands?

Hildegard: No, Dear, you are safe in God's sanctuary. What is your name?

Sigewize: I do not know. I have no name. I am earth and dust and stars and death. Save poor Sigewize.

Hildegard: Who is she?

Sigewize: A girl, she travels with me, sometimes good, sometimes bad. I protect her with my knife, to keep the strong ones away.

Hildegard: She will be safe here, too.

Sigewize: Will you stay with us, Mother, and care for us?

Hildegard: I will, Dear. Don't be afraid. God stays with us here, and He will be with you hereafter.

Sigewize: Hold me, Mother. Keep out the night and the wind.

Hildegard: The living light is with us and, if we call on her, she will keep us warm.

Hildegard wrapped the girl in her arms and half guided, half carried her back to the infirmary. Elsewhere in the abbey Kuno fumed at himself as his secretary tried to keep a crowd of pilgrims from entering the abbot's study.

Kuno: Pilgrims, pilgrims, pilgrims. At least I have the satisfaction that with her will go her wretched, dusty pilgrims, while their alms will stay with me. And yet I could love her. For all her simplicity she carries a gentility, the mark of an old family. We will dwell the poorer in sympathy if the richer in calm, the surer of

> solitude though the poorer of spirit. Steel yourself, Abbot; time's sword will fall for her, as it surely must for you.

When the secretary could no longer stop them, assorted pilgrims interrupted Kuno's solitude. Following them through the door Bernard calmly waited his turn, his wry smile threatening to become an outright grin. Kuno had thrown his tall, thin frame into a chair. He stroked his chin as though he were training a beard to a sharp point and glared at the first to address him.

> **Pilgrim:** We would see the sainted Lady, Milord. We beg boons of healing, advice, and prayer.
>
> **Kuno:** Not yet sainted, and a simple nun, hardly a lady any longer sincer her tithing. But you may see her as you wish. She seems to smell your suit, as I do, for even now she comes to you.

Though the crowd had nearly filled the room, Hildegard managed to enter, bowing to the abbot, and approach, as they made room for her. Seeing her, Kuno rose, feeling suddenly an inescapable desire to exit the room.

> **Hildegard:** So many . . . but since they are the Lord's, so are they mine. I will tend them, Abbot.
>
> **Kuno:** So you will, and take them with you to Rupertsberg along with my blessing.

As Kuno stalked out past Bernard's raised finger, the pilgrims gathered round her, begging her help with this pain and that sorrow, when their words rained too heavily, she closed her eyes, lowered her head, and raised her hand. With their silence she asked them to accompany her to the infirmary: they fell into line like eager but obedient schoolchildren. As she turned to exit, she spotted Bernard, bowed to him, shrugged, and motioned for him to follow. He laughed, and once the pilgrims had followed the abbess, he too fell in line.

At the infirmary Hildegard stooped to attend the sick, one by one. Bernard joined her, blessing some, laying his hands on fevered foreheads, and helping the abbess mix her medicines. As they worked together, he was gradually able to explain to her who he was and why he had come.

Hildegard: What brings you to us, good Father?

Bernard: You bring me, Abbess. I have heard of your holy works and have read your holy words at the synod in Rome. I am Bernard of Clairvaux and have come to talk with you and receive your blessing.

Hildegard: I should receive blessing from you, Milord Abbot.

Bernard: No, no: just a commoner, a creature like yourself, born of and to God. Will we have a chance to talk?

Hildegard: We can talk as we bless and mix medicines. If we're patient with these pilgrims, we may walk to yonder hill overlooking the river and pointing to Rupertsberg, where tomorrow I serve my own abbey. Will you see it with me?

Bernard: That I will. But first we tend.

He said a prayer and slowly crossed himself over a patient, and then Bernard turned his attention fully on Hildegard. He absorbed her demeanor, observed her ability with her patients, and any doubts that might have afflicted him at the synod in Rome departed as lightly as motes in a sunbeam. Together they had worked the sunbeams to sleep, and before they had finished, the night had also given up its hold on the air, so that dawn just brushed the morning with its rosy glow. When they had seen each petitioner, they climbed wearily together the path above the abbey and look out over the valley.

> Hildegard: Here they nestle, the convent above and the streets of the town below, Rupertsberg, by Bingen.
>
> Bernard: Lovely it is, lovely as your visions of our Lord and Savior.
>
> Hildegard: Lovely from the Lord, and occasionally hellish of the devil, but we are vessels and must allow ourselves be filled with what the Lord pours. See the life below: even in the barest morning they already begin their labors—funny thought, since we have worked all night?

Below, the street filled with folk: farmers with their wares, craftsmen, soldiers, pilgrims, the clowns and performers singing, dancing, playing their simple instruments, hoping for the orts of someone's cast-off breakfast. As Hildegard and Bernard watched them, tiny in the distance, Keunegard sidled up unnoticed, following them and watching with them the scenes in the streets. She hid herself quietly in some brush beside the way. As Bernard spoke, he waved a roundish finger in the air before him, as if he were drawing what he saw.

> Bernard: The hills circle the town, and the river splits the middle: a bowlful of life in the shape of the *theta*, that reminds us of death. We at once live and die, mortal, born again to God.
>
> Hildegard: Death means life—we serve awhile and then go joyfully—and life means death, and life in death: we go too soon, but we go to God.

Bernard: Do you not wish that we could see Him come again, that we could live in that time? Such glory, descending from the clouds on angels' wings amid the fire and tumult.

Hildegard: Already fire and tumult, sickness, revolution, war, the nature of the world, consume our children, and each day dies with Christ's coming, within if not without, in pain or in prayer. See how His children dance, while His Horsemen wait at their door, they blithe as mendicant clouds. But let them live, Hildegard! I judge too harshly. We are all, in our own way, God's prophets, whether we preach, dance, shoe horses, pick grapes, or suffer visions.

Bernard: Suffer indeed?

Hildegard: Though joyfully. The visions bring beauty with pain. I will mourn the passing of this beautiful world, its rivers of topaz, emerald bays, glowing vineyards, bright, motive viridity, and yet I long for my own death and resurrection, to gaze peacefully on the face of God and leave healing to the One who heals all.

Bernard: But yet we live, and I must keep you no longer from your charges. Let us return through the garden so we may smell the lilacs. Their scent may serve us nearly as well as sleep.

As Hildegard and Bernard tramped back to the hall, Keunegard emerged from her hiding place, her mind astir with the many troubles of the folk that disturbed the peace of the nuns' seclusion. Fascinated with the height of the path above the town, she peered over the edge, stepped just back, and twirled in circles, her robe wheeling, her toes inches away from slipping from the path.

Keunegard: Golgotha, death and damnation, rebirth and resurrection. Come, Lord Jesus, I cannot wait for you. Shall I die? Shall I die? Ah! I hear her screams from the sepulchre. Lamblike she cries, and I must stay for her.

She flung back her head with her arms stretched wide, then dashed down the path toward the infirmary.

There, in the women's ward Sigewize lay restrained, crying so loudly that her voice echoed down the valley. In the men's ward, Volmar, Hildegard's secretary, lay nursing a fever. The nuns tended them and a score and more other patients.

Sigewize: Out, out, Devil! Your own horns gall you. No! You will not have me. Put down your trident. Blow the horns and call God's bleeding angels. Beelzebub!

Hearing the screams, Hildegard, though exhausted, entered to assist as she could. She sat down next to Volmar, mopped first her brow with a corner of her robe, then his with a cool cloth. She fought off her lip's intention to tremble.

Clementia: She has been kicking and thrashing, the girl. I will hold her down.

Hildegard: She must have fresh air. And keep fresh fir sprigs about her. I believe she is free of demons. Now we must wait for the fever to break. Irmengard, bring feverfew in boiled water. Volmar, now tell me what are you doing here? Needing a bit of holiday?

Irmengard: He has taken ill suddenly. He watched the last nights with the acrobat Dayadva, oh, and the old pilgrim who carried the cross in the marketplace, whom the monks have lately buried.

Hildegard: He has borne his cross, more so than he has let on, but we must yet bear ours. How are you, old Friend? Can you speak?

Volmar: Healthy as an angel two days old, and will be fine again, but just now I have the weight of God's earth upon me.

Hildegard: Our mortality, Dear Brother, from which God frees us—but you must spend many days with us yet. Our work: what would I do without you? You pray for me, guide me, and write for me. You are my mouth and hands to the larger world.

Volmar: This little life stricken through by a cross serves you with its last breath. As the circle crossed turned this life to God and you, so it brings the soul to God at last.

Hildegard: Not so quickly, my friend, too quick to go. With you goes work and brotherhood. Clementia, he must not lie here with the other sick. Take him to private quarters among the monks. The young woman has calmed now and will be all right without you.

Clementia: Your voice seems to have calmed her. I will tend to the monk.

Volmar: I came to serve you and go your servant. God bless your visions and bring you scribes sufficient for your teeming mind.

Hildegard: What it bears will be both yours and mine. May it find welcome in God's eyes.

Volmar: God go with you.

Hildegard: And with you.

Too soon to God, beloved Brother, Hildegard thought, as Clementia went for monks to carry Volmer to his own cell, where they could watch over him in quiet.

Hildegard then passed to the women's ward to check on the mad girl, taking a cup from Irmengard to try to help Sigewize to drink. When she sat with the girl, she demanded of herself that she keep her own features absolutely, reassuringly calm, despte her worry for Volmar.

> **Hildegard:** Daughter, are you resting now? Please sip this.
>
> **Sigewize:** My eyes are clearing. Who are you, blessed Mother?
>
> **Hildegard:** God's servant, my dear, and yours as physician. Do you remember your name?
>
> **Sigewize:** My name is Sigewize; I came from . . . I cannot remember.
>
> **Hildegard:** Rest, child; you are safe with us.
>
> **Sigewize:** I will stay with you and serve you. Please let me. God loves you. What are you?
>
> **Irmengard:** She is our abbess, and we are her nuns.
>
> **Sigewize:** Then I too will stay and be your nun. I feel faint.
>
> **Hildegard:** Rest, dear, and drink this, then sleep. We must find your family. We will have time enough to talk about your future. Rest.

Clementia returned to the infirmary, her hands clasped in front of her.

Clementia: The monk Volmar is dying. You may want to attend him. We hadn't even time to move him.

Hildegard: Swiftly as a breath the angel comes. How briefly I had a brother, son, friend to my heart and to the words that come to me from God. He saw as I spoke and wrote as I heard. May God give him clear sight in the company of seraphim. This too-small wretched globe cracks with a moment and dies before a pen stroke can purchase reprieve for body or soul. I will see him reanimated. God save us all.

Clementia: Amen.

Irmengard: Shall I tend the young lady?

Hildegard: Bring her a fresh robe to wear and bread if she can eat, and learn what you can about her family. Perhaps speaking in safety will help clear her mind.

Irmengard: (Helping Sigewize.) Come, dear, carefully.

Hildegard: We reap that God may harvest: one soul flown to God, one soul won for God.

Crossing herself and gathering what strength she could find within herself, Hildegard returned to her old Friend Volmar. He lay stretched flat and quiet, with barely the energy to open his eyes. Against the reddish hue of Hildegard's hand, Volmar's fingers looked grey and bloodless.

Hildegard: At last you have grown tired, Brother, and shirk your duties in the infirmary and the scriptorium.

Volmar: I believe I have but one duty left, my Sister, and that is to die.

Hildegard: Not today, old friend: today is a day to live, to walk among the birches and whistle with the river birds. Today is a healing day, to set broken bones and cool fevers, to turn the young loose upon the world, and to record visions of glory.

Volmar: I hope soon to have a vision of glory beyond recording. I only wish that, when I see it, I could see it with you.

Hildegard: Our time will come after many days, and perhaps we shall walk together in the gardens of Heaven. Come, Brother, will you not talk with me? Will you rise and walk in our own garden? Will you pray?

Volmar: Yes, let us pray the Our Father. I have little strength. Kuno has come to see me.

Hildegard: No wonder your strength fails. You do not need an abbot; you need the summer air and green hills and your old friend to talk to.

Volmar: Our Father . . .

Hildegard: And Mother, and Brother, Rose, Dove, Manna, Lamb, Voice, Truth, and Living Light, come and raise this poor malingerer to share Your praise. Your will . . .

Volmar: Be done.

Hildegard: . . . binds us blood and bone as family in your house. Come lift this best of brothers from his bed to your viridity.

Volmar: Forgive us our trespasses. Amen.

Hildegard: Amen. How many times have we walked, Volmar, in the garden or by the river, and how many times have we talked of verses and of visions? Do you remember when you took robe and tonsure and I took habit? We were nearly of an age, too young to know what we were doing, but sure we were doing right, and how many times since in fast or prayer or illness we have known God's love and healing power and the rightness of our lives. But if our lives had been different, another age, another place, another world, what then might we have been or done or shared, meeting each other on the road or in the marketplace or amid a field of daisies? (She turns to him, and he is dead.) Too quick, too fragile. You should have waited. Oh my, my, my. My friend, what will I do without you? May angels dress your feet with ermine and lift your eager steps to God. Oh, my. How can I?—I cannot say good-bye.

ぞ ぞ ぞ

Some days later, in the afternoon, among the Rupertsberg streets, Adelheid and Damyata strolled together. Despite the shyness their places in life demanded of them, they had felt, from that first meeting, drawn to each other. Young though they were, they had at first opportunity fallen into conversation about the nothings that so fascinate us when we don't care what we say, wishing only to hear each other's voice. Adelheid's glance strayed to Damyata's thick, curly black hair, and Damyata required all his strength to keep himself from simply gazing into the girl's sky-blue eyes.

Damyata: You have seen show.

Adelheid: So beautiful, lively, full of color.

Damyata: Like you. Why you wear black? You should wear colors, bright and many, like the flowers on the hillside.

> Adelheid: I am a nun. We wear black to remind us of the brevity of life, the simplicity of our days, and our dedication to the service of God.
>
> Damyata: God not mind if you wear yellow and green, like His own hills and flowers. They too serve.
>
> Adelheid: You do not understand.
>
> Damyata: Yes, I do not understand.

They talked, their thoughts eager and random as the breeze, as the clouds rolled by. Lost in their conversation, they hardly noticed the group of monks and sweating laborers who crossed their path, moving furniture. Thunder sounded in the distance.

> Monk: Cover the furniture: the rain will ruin it.
>
> 1st Man: Thank God it's only nuns we're moving and few belongings.
>
> Monk: Your labor serves God, much or little.
>
> 2nd Man: Much if I must, little if I may, and then a mug of beer.
>
> Monk: You'll have your mug of beer soon enough. God's labor first, and it's little enough to ask of you.
>
> 2nd Man: Six days' labor, and quite a birthing, if you ask me, for it weren't delivered till four thousand years later.
>
> Monk: Is that how long you take in your delivery, four thousand years?
>
> 2nd Man: Extrapolation doesn't become you, Milord Monk, and you'll see the labor done tooth sweet for something for the sweet tooth after.
>
> 1st Man: Sausage and cakes—and beer.

Monk: All you can eat, Burgher, and drink, Meister, if you can get the furniture to the convent before yonder rain clouds flood us all downstream to Paris.

2nd Man: Bay if you will, Sir Monk; this murky clay will let us move no faster than if we were Cain and Abel themselves.

Monk: Little able, as I can see, and a good caning would not hurt you.

2nd Man: Hurt it would, and make double oxes of us both, since our wives has done it once already.

Monk: A good man will know a good woman and ward her all the days of his life.

2nd Man: A good monk will know a good man and reward him before the last day of his life.

Monk: Food and pay when day is done; for better pay, look to heaven's King. Hurry and follow along. I'm going ahead. You lumber like cripples. Come on!

2nd Man: His lumber will cripple us. Long may Heaven's King reign, and long will it rain before we see pay from this slaving monk in this world.

1st Man: So I believe.

As the laborers finally entered the abbey hall, Hildegard, Bernard, and Sigewize tentatively emerged together, checking for rain.

Hildegard: I believe, Father Bernard, you prosecuted our cause with the Abbot and opened the door for our move to Rupertsberg, and I would not doubt you swayed the king as well.

Bernard: God opens doors; we but grease the hinges. I serve the cloth, not the court, and the Church, not its hierarchy. Too often we are like mosquitoes living off others' blood, tossed to live or die in the carelessness of fate's whirlwind.

Hildegard: You surprise me, Father; you don't believe in fate.

Bernard: I believe that some men believe in it, and that when God's breath blows us here or there, we choose by what we wish fate wills rather than by what we fear God wills. And you, Young doe, Sigewize, you are too lovely to confine yourself in a convent. Find a husband and have children.

Sigewize: No husband! I want only to serve God and my lady the abbess. He cured my soul, and she my body, and I would serve others as I have been served. Please, Mother, you will take me in?

Bernard: God offers many paths of service, to increase his Church being one of them.

Sigewize: I hope to increase the good works of His Church by so much as one poor girl may. Please permit me, Father. I am happy here and have nowhere else to go.

Bernard: You could learn nothing of her family?

Hildegard: Nothing.

Bernard: Then she has no dowry. The Church will not take her unless she can pay to enter.

Hildegard: They will take her because they will take her. They must take her. Where else can she go? Do I not bring in enough in alms and gifts to pay a dowry many times over? I am not so unaware of the world as you may think, Father.

Bernard turned his kind but stern eyes upon the girl. He took her small hand in his soft, cool fingers and spoke gently but firmly.

Bernard: If you serve, serve because you will, not because you must, because you choose, not because you have no choice.

Sigewize: I have learned to love God and will love and serve His abbess all the days of my life.

Bernard: I sought not to dissuade you, but to test your resolve. Welcome to His Church, and God bless your choosing.

Sigewize: Thank you, Milord Father.

Hildegard: Welcome, Sister and Daughter. We will arrange for your study and later for your confirmation. Go now to Clementia and ask her to clothe you appropriately. Thank you, Father. Will we see you again?

Bernard: In the life to come, yes, my dear Sister, where spirit, flesh, wish and world make one. But for now I must go, and I hope this rag of a cloak will hold off the rain. Blessings, Sister, and good-bye!

Hildegard watched Bernard disappear down the road, then turned her eyes and thoughts to Rupertsberg, which seemed to her to swirl below in the mist of light rain. There the acrobats, beneath the cover of some trees, considered their course.

Datta: Not the same without Dayadva.

Dall: How could it be? He held us like butter to bread together.

Damyata: But he has won us the Great Lady's blessing.

Datta: If you do not lose it by making eyes at her nuns. Anyway, blessing does not make bread or cheese. Maybe we should settle and work, pick grapes, build roads, make shoes.

Dall: What do we know about grapes or roads or shoes?

Datta: I know that we have no grapes to eat and no shoes to wear and many roads to walk.

Damyata: Grandfather, Mother, we are cobblers or acrobats? Grandfather, you taught us well, and God has given us nothing but dances. Let us do as He calls us and be what He made us.

Datta: And the child shall lead them. You are I believe right, Damyata, your father still with us, smart and strong. But I am old. How much longer can I dance?

Damyata: Till you can dance no more. Then you will teach others to dance.

Dall: So the dance will go on even when we cannot, and we will please and serve even when we have gone. We will be ourselves till we cannot, and then we shall meet Dayadva again. And you, my son, I believe have a reason to remain here to dance?

Damyata: Mother! I think only that we have no need now to travel, and for Father's sake reason to stay and remember.

Datta: Amen.

Dall and Damyata: Amen.

The rain fell softly throughout the day, and the sky punctuated each hour of the night with vigorous thunder. Next morning at the abbey the sun shone brightly again, and the pools of rainwater soon sunk into the ground, leaving only a glistening dew. The sisters, having sung morning prayers, sat for a moment in the warm light of the garden.

> Adelheid: The wind through apples and arbors smells sweet as paradise here.
>
> Clementia: Because it is our own wind, unbreathed by monkish drones. The abbot's face as we left was pursed as a peach pit. There's an ill wind that blows no one good.
>
> Hildegard: Yet, as an abbot, he deserves our respect. But peachpit does nicely.
>
> Irmengard: All arrangements have been made, our quarters are furnished, and the new infirmary is prepared. We have only to complete the courtyard for waiting visitors, on which I hope we may spend years. I have always loved a garden.
>
> Hildegard: Where is Richardis?
>
> Irmengard: She was to bring Sister Keunegard, but the abbot detained her.
>
> Hildegard: The ill wind must blow up its last storm.

Keunegard broke in on their ease, flailing her arms and moaning. Hildegard rose and held her hands out to welcome her. Keunegard stopped, speaking rapidly, tugging at her fingers.

> Keunegard: The sea rages, and the earth vomits up its dead. Moths fly from the linden tree and cover the staring moon.
>
> Hildegard: What troubles you, my dear?

Keunegard: They come, Blessed Mother, they come, but not for long. He is a viper, and his words are toads to plague us.

Richardis and several monks entered from the main hall.

Richardis: Do not ask me; I cannot speak.

Monk: Milady Abbess, you are to know that Sister Richardis has been elected to her own abbey and will serve henceforth as Abbess of Bassum in Bremen. Her mother, the Marchioness of Stade, and her brother, Archbishop Hartwig, will soon arrive to take her. May we all wish her well in her new post.

Hildegard: So from the garden the serpent takes our children. How brief paradise! But God himself has shown me her place is here. Her own family has betrayed us, I guess. Nobility of blood will set nobility of place above nobility of soul. Church nor state may countermand God's plan. If she does not want to leave me, I will not have her taken. The stones and trees themselves will give her sanctuary, warding off those who would come to steal her. His angels' halberds will bar the door. I feel the fire of God upon me and know that it must be so.

Richardis: I do not know what to say, Mother, if I have been given to you only to be taken away when you need me most. Does God make such playthings of us?

Hildegard: Not God, but men, and maybe women, too, who would use us to their glory rather than God's. How can they match their will against God's? How can they? Can they not see His fiery hand poised like a sword above their heads? Ach, we are all guilty.

Can I have misunderstood? Hildegard thought. Did I mistake my own wishes for God's, my fancy for God's graced vision? And as she thought, she felt pressure behind her eyes, and then she saw a whirling rainbow of color. A vision, the figure of Jutta, her mentor and friend, emerged from the pain.

> **Spirit of Jutta: Beloved daughter, you must do as the Church requires of you. We are bricks in God's road, paving the way to Rome. Abbot and archbishop guide us on the path. We must serve humbly; even an abbess should do so. But do not doubt your visions or their source; through them you should strengthen your faith! This wheel of a world turns, and visions clear the path to His right hand.**

The vision faded in a burst of color and pain, dissolving into throbbing ribbons. I know how to believe, but not what to believe, and I trust God, but not myself, Hildegard thought. Like anyone else, I am dust at last, and what the spirit wills, the flesh may fail to perform. Then she turned to Richardis, summoning speech and wiping a strand of blond hair from her friend's temple.

> **Richardis: You have pain, Mother?**

> **Hildegard: It passes. As the world calls us we must go, so we walk in God's light. Can we call the day or the night a moment sooner than they come by their own nature? Dearest Richardis, you *are* viridity, God's growing shoot rising from the belly of His earth to proclaim His name through the air, to seed His church with the love that calls the spirit to Him. We serve at His call. I will care for my nuns, and another shall record my visions, and you will guide your own flock as our Church calls you to do.**

Richardis: What about you? What about my own visions? I do not see falling stars, flaming angels, grasping demons, nor do I hear the inwrought music of the spheres, but I know as I know my name or your love that God wills me serve you here in this our hard-won abbey. Shall a daughter leave the mother of her spirit, the wellspring of her heart?

Hildegard: Mind, heart, soul spring from God, who attends wherever you go, as will my hourly prayers. Who part in flesh need never part in spirit.

As they spoke Archbishop Hartwig and the Marchioness of Stade, Richardis' brother and mother, arrived with their mandate. Their strides noble and stately, they wasted no words, addressing the nuns with practiced authority.

Marchioness: Obedient Daughter, how long since I have seen you! You blossom in the service of your Church, and you should thank this abbess who has trained you to service beyond her station.

Hartwig: Dutiful Sister, Sister twice over, we have given much labor to winning you this post where your own talents may shine as befits your family. Come with us now. Bremen awaits you, and your work allows no delay. You will minister to a noble folk and nobly merit God's reward.

Richardis: Mother, Brother, I would serve God nobly in the humblest of circumstances and, I hope, would earn God's reward were I a milkmaid or a queen.

Marchioness: He saw fit to make you neither, and you may thank him for it. Come now: no delay.

At a loss, Richardis turned to her mother, then to her mentor and friend.

> Richardis: Dearest True Mother, my abbess and friend, I doubt whether this event serves me or God. I have sometimes wished for such a chance, yet now that it finds me, I doubt my desire of it. Leaving pulls the hair from the root, or as the Spaniard says, the nail from the finger. People will err and have their way, God's wish be what it will. If I must go, and I cannot serve you in fact, I will serve you in prayer. Think of me, and bless my sisters for me.
>
> Hartwig: Richardis, preferment awaits.
>
> Richardis: No greater service will I do than I have done. I would say "God be with you," spiritual mother, but I know already that He is.

With a curt bow to the abbess, the noble pair led their kinswoman away. Richardis barely had the will to turn her head for one last look at her friend and mentor.

They scarcely left Richardis time for packing. Within minutes Hildegard, who had wandered toward the public hallway, heard their carriage moving briskly away down the abbey road. She thought in that moment less of Richardis than of herself, and her mind turned to all the lonely people of the world, lost in a sense of loss, caught in the quicksand of feelings of abandonment.

> Hildegard: My mouth was stopped, or I should have cried heaven for reprieve. God go with you also, beloved Daughter, and angels tend your abbey to protect you from bishops and kings, life and death, and the fruit and the chaff of this world. And may God help me when I am lonely and bring me a hand to record

> His visions. Ah, again I see: it is the marketplace, and there among the merchants is the worm, drawn by the aroma of virtue. Yes: it is the dragon, full of seeping wounds, trodden by virtue, but bleeding madness into the world. The head is trampled, the eyes bloodshot, but the ears hear, and the fangs remain full of poison. Hands it has to grasp, a voice to deceive, the voice of Pride, and flames pour from its mouth. Woe to the one who hears that voice, who feels those flames! Yet I must ask myself: how much do I feel God's anger, and how much do I fail to still my own?

Sharing her sorrow, the other nuns sought their abbess to give and get what comfort they could, each feeling in her heart of hearts the sting of friendship that no person can fully share with another.

> Irmengard: Have we missed Richardis? I wanted to say good-bye.
>
> Hildegard: (Coming out of her trance as Irmengard comes to comfort her). She sends you all her blessings.
>
> Adelheid: We will miss her.
>
> Keunegard: Satan takes her from us. God bless her and save us all.
>
> All: Amen.

Adelheid began to sing the first lines of a song from *Ordo Virtutum*, the "Song of the Virgins," partly in instinctive response to her teacher, partly to still the fleeting thoughts of her own mind. The tune rose, fluttered, floated gently as butterflies.

> "O Virginitas, in regali thalamo stas.
> How sweetly you burn in the Royal embrace
> When the sun enflames your face.
> May your blooms never fall!"

The others joined in her simple but elegant plainsong, until Hildegard grew wobbly on her feet.

Clementia: Abbess, you look deathly pale.

Hildegard: Nonsense, I am quite all right. Let us sing a prayer for our sister, who leaves her loving family for another loving family loving . . .

Before they could catch her, Hildegard fainted.

Adelheid: Abbess!

Clementia: We must get her to bed. With all the fuss, this loss of Richardis has proven too much for her.

Irmengard: What should I do? Without the abbess or Sister Richardis to tell me, I do not know what medicines to prepare.

Clementia: We must fare as best we can. Bring something hot . . . and something cold, and we will hope she regains consciousness soon to guide us.

They carried her limp body, heavy with unconsciousness, to the infirmary, while in the opposite side of Disibodenberg Abbey, in the abbot's office, by the low and hazy light that crept through chinks in the covered window, Kuno sat nodding over his work, dreaming, allowing himself to drift between sleep and waking. His thoughts leapt and lingered, chaotic as grasshoppers, from repairs to provisions for his monks to contracted masses to letters from the Bishop to alms for the town's poor to controversies over details of the Rule to what his life might have been had he been born a first son, but inevitably they alit on the woman who at once inspired and plagued him. He fought with his own prayers as they wavered between wishing her a long, saintly life and a quick and merciful death, all, of course, as God willed.

For two weeks Hildegard lay feverish, and for two more weeks, tended by her faithful flock, she suffered convalescence, and when she felt ready, a horse-drawn carriage took her with her nuns to Rupertsberg.

※ ※ ※

As he learned of her recovery, Kuno sat on a bench musing, his head resting against the cool of the stone wall that separated the shady side of the garden and the abbot's office. For a time he considered the true nature of vision, devotion, and prayer.

> Kuno: A mountain. He sits atop it, light flowing from the palms of his hands. Another stands at the base of the mountain. He is dressed in a coat of eyes, eyes that gather in the light.

As Kuno drifted off to sleep, a vision of Hildegard invaded his dream.

> Hildegard: That is Fear-of-God gathering the light of Christ.
>
> Kuno: Yes. And a young girl stands there, smiling, dressed in white.
>
> Hildegard: That is the poor in spirit. They look to the kingdom of heaven. So was I when I came to your abbey.
>
> Kuno: Youthful, simple, eager. Full of light. And something probing in your eyes. Look now at the Man on the mountain. How the rays of light fall from Him like rain.
>
> Hildegard: Those are the virtues, granted us by Christ.

Kuno: I must sit beneath and be touched by them. They are so beautiful! They are . . . But you, Sister: why are you here?

A Monk entered to wake Kuno. He pushed aside the window shutter and lit a candle against the grey afternoon. Kuno sat still, unwilling to turn his eyes back toward the dream or forward toward the flickering light.

Monk: Milord Kuno: news of the nun Richardis.

Kuno: What? How dare you! Oh. She was dispatched to Bremen. This time even Mainz and the pope himself align with us against our enemy.

Monk: She went tearfully, but truly, and she has taken up her new post. The Marchioness and the Archbishop send their greetings and thanks.

Kuno: She must obey, she shall obey, and we shall rule this time. For once the woman must obey authority. At last in this point, finally, she shall not have her own way. And have we any more pilgrims at our doorstep?

Monk: They have all been redirected for Rupertsberg, to the Abbess Hildegard, as your lordship will recall.

Kuno: You have done your duty to God and me. You may go.

Monk: Thank you, Milord Abbot.

Kuno: One moment yet: have the monks prepare to sing a *Requiem* and a *Te Deum*, praising a dead time past and a newborn time to come.

As the monk exited, Kuno allowed the moment of quiet to help him shape thoughts to wash the dream of that woman's voice from his memory.

Kuno: Peace, peace. My monastery rings with a male silence that whispers to the dead of long winters till resurrection and to the living of sleep-like devotions uninterrupted by the knock and clamor of the world. Money comes to us from Rupertsberg in trust, and we may disperse it as we will. We will repair the chapel and order a marble font from the best craftsmen of Venice and send to Milan for albs and vestments warm and cheery for a winter's mass and up the Rhine for old wine to bless a summer compline. Now the monastery feels as it should, quiet, secluded, the old, sharp smell of camphor covered with the odor of earth, the cry of pilgrims sacrificed to the sigh of wind over the stones. Did I say *sacrificed*? I may not tell even God that I would give up the robes, the wine, the peace for a vision of my own, a voice, a cloudy censer, a spark from the footfall of a passing cherub to draw from me a proving tear of speechlessness. Am I locked now in my own darkness, without my troublesome saint, without gall and food for complaint to give cause for the angry envy that consumes me in this self-imposed grave? Well, then, I will serve beautiful mass until the hour I die, when visionless life ends, and St. Peter must wrestle me from the gates. From there I may see, if only in a glimpse before falling, the longed-for face of God.

The monk returned, interrupting Kuno's revery.

Monk: The song is prepared, Milord.

Kuno: Have the monks take once a day a turn through Rupertsberg, singing a *Gloria Patri* in delight at our nuns' passing—departure, that is. They at least will not forget us, though they have shed us. Though the wasp die in stinging, he may gain small revenge with the pain of his sting and then fertilize the ground with his corpse. Let us go then, we two.

At the Rupertsberg convent, still incompletely constructed, the nuns tended their patients in their new clean, airy Infirmary. One particular patient dwelt first in their thoughts and prayers, one whose illness had not healed.

Irmengard: She lay there many days without reprieve. Once she got well enough to move, even the short journey here proved too much for her fragile health. Now her forehead will not cool and she cannot eat. She barely speaks, except in fear of what she sees: something of God's retribution upon her. Can you imagine that? Retribution on one of the Church's living saints, humble as the roadside violet, sweetly healing as the mint-sprig at the white willow's horned feet.

Clementia: I should long since have walked to Bremen and carried Sister here on my own back, rather than see this illness eat away our abbess's body and soul.

Irmengard: God will not have her slack. A saint must remain in all acts a saint and must not stray a hairsbreadth from His will.

Clementia: And what if this Man-Church sacrifice her honor and God's will to play the sycophant to dukes and kings? We should ourselves take sword and flail to these bishops till they hear the prophet's words.

Irmengard: If Richardis were here, she would caution you not to flay the Church, but to understand that we are servants born to carry medicines and prayer beads rather than swords. Remember, too, that the position of her family had much to do with their decision: the noble folk have their own duties beyond our knowledge.

Clementia: She is not here, and I fear our losing our abbess as well as our sister, and I would lay some stripes across some tender backs before I would see these saints go unavenged and those sinners go unscathed.

Irmengard: Revenge is mine, says the Lord.

Clementia: You need not quote me scripture, Sister. My only desire is to be His instrument, not His counselor. You will excuse me.

Adelheid: Here is the tea, Sister Irmengard. We have given her so many doses that I doubt its effect, but I have become quite skillful at preparing it. Would you like me to watch her for a while so you may rest?

Keunegard, as usual lurking unobserved in the shadows, sat to listen, her eyes and ears intent, her mind unfocusable in its chaotic ramblings.

Irmengard: No, dear, thank you. You go sleep. I will tend her for a bit, Adelheid. Abbess and Sister, I am a shadow without you. I live for your looks and guidance and for the glimpse of God I find in your eyes and voice. I am no Richardis, I know, with her fiery eyes and welling mind, but I love you as a blood-sister should, even more than I should for one devoted to otherworldly things. But you are more of the next world than this one, so I need feel little guilt, I deem. I wish I knew more to do to help you now. I wish Mother were here to help us both. Can I do nothing to keep you with me a little longer? Must I live alone in the world, shorn of kin and kindness? I feel a long life ahead, and I do not want to live it without you. Come, some tea, perhaps. Day nears. The nightingale long since ended its song, and the lark takes up matins. Do you love me enough to endure this life with me?

Hildegard: Who sits with me? Irmengard?

Irmengard: Blessed voice and eyes return to me.

Hildegard: What visions I have had. Have I long been sick?

Irmengard: Long. Do not rise too quickly. Rest.

Hildegard: I must rise and prepare. A message is coming.

Irmengard: What message?

Hildegard: We will soon see, though I fear it will shake the abbey stones and send us spinning to the river below. Oh, I am dizzy. I thought, my dear, that I had been wrong, that I had imposed my own sight on God's visions, that I would keep Richardis from her abbey for my sake, because we here love her and wanted her to stay. But these dreams in my sickness scream that I should have kept her though I needed tooth and claw to do so.

Keunegard: Alas, Richardis!

Irmengard: The devil speaks.

Hildegard: No, no, only our poor Keunegard. Maybe she sees what I see, and she can't bear it. God save you, dear one.

Keunegard, startling Irmengard, rushed to her abbess, petted her head, and placed her own head in Hildegard's lap.

Keunegard: Poor Mother, poor Sister, too. God holds you from Satan's fingers, but the evil one has touched our sister, and the shadow has taken her quick. God save us. God save us!

Irmengard: Poor sister—I must remove her so you can rest.

Hildegard: Not necessary. Far worse comes soon, if I am not mistaken.

As Hildegard spoke, they could hear a monk's footfalls in the corridor outside the Infirmary. He strode in quickly and address the nuns formally.

Monk: Forgive me for disturbing in your sickness, Abbess: Archbishop Henry of Mainz sends to tell you that Abbess Richardis of Bremen has died of a sudden illness. He regrets that the Church may not better heed your visions and reminds you that we are all human and therefore dust. Condolences, Milady.

Hildegard: Hardly a lady, nearly dust. So I foresaw. So weary this life, ill in sickness or in health, which takes its best and gentlest at the height of their service to God and us. We crawl on our bellies, feeding on dust even as we pray. We must curse God or fall upon His mercies.

Keunegard: Alas, our sister! Her soul calls and crushes me!

Hildegard: Calm, perturbed spirit. We must cleanse this sickness, too. God has shown me once again the truth

> of His visions, and our sister's soul sings orisons for us now till we meet her in Heaven. We must endure. Please call Clementia to help me to the chapel.

Irmengard, in tears, followed the monk out. Fear-of-God, a figure that dogged Hildegard's visions, dressed in a dark cloak that covered her from toes to crown, entered the abbess's thoughts.

> **Fear-of-God:** You have only God's visions. The rest is illusion.
>
> **Hildegard:** What can I do when even visions are not enough? I can only advise, not compel.
>
> **Fear-of-God:** Think not of the ends, only of His guidance.
>
> **Keunegard:** Who comes? He has stolen my eyes, so I cannot see.
>
> **Fear-of-God:** You are a vessel. Serve him well.

As mysteriously as it had appeared, the vision vanished.

> **Hildegard:** She is gone now. Come, help me up. We will help each other.

A season of unusual cold and rain followed, and then a winter of deep snows. The nuns never entirely recovered from the loss of Richardis, and many of them struggled in their own prayers with a sense of guilt at the lingering desire to place blame. They prayed singly and together, sang singly and together, and remembered as the world around them lost the echo of their dirge in its own celebration of spring and renewal.

Chapter Three

Death, the intimate of everyone of that age, seldom left the people's sides or their thoughts. Daily activity offered a respite, not an analgesic; anodyne they found only in their conviction, to the degree that they had it, that God should one day mend their bodies and cleanse their souls.

In the cathedrals that had begun to punctuate European towns, when skies would clear, pouring light over them like balmy rain, or when their bishops, perched above in their seats of power, spoke out kindnesses or the excision of some small suffering, they found moments of palpable praise. Through the quotidian labor in the fields or quarries, in the trades, in forced or poverty-imposed servitude, they bore what their souls and bodies could. Finally they found a brief, quiet grave before, a generation or two later, their bones were dug up to make space for another, tossed in the common dust of the charnel house, mixed in osteo-matrices for Christ to disentangle with His Second Coming. Such were the meditations of the thinking class, the distant dreams of the souls who made bread tromping through the muck, harvesting or planting grain, or wielding mattocks.

In the Rupertsberg streets, too, folk found their common humanity. On holiday weeks they played their religious drama on the backs of wagons in the marketplace or outside the church or cathedral. Their plays gradually grew to comprise whole cycles, encompassing the world from Creation to Apocalypse. In an early version of one such play, beneath the flatbed upon which the craftsmen-characters dutifully acted their parts, sat a painted hell-mouth from which poured their fellows to grimace and roar among the audience upon the ground, acting the part of the obligatory, semi-comic demons.

Following them came a grand and strutting Satan, dressed as a Roman Centurion, who posed before the crowd and called in stentorian voice to his human comrade and fellow actor.

> **Satan:** What would you have me do, great Herod?
>
> **Herod:** I must not have my rule challenged by man or boy. Send the soldiers into Jerusalem. Have them destroy every male child two years of age and younger. Leave none living. Be quick and bloody. This newborn king must not reign. I will live supreme for ever, save Caesar, of course. And while you're at it, bring me a fresh crop of virgins, too.
>
> **Satan:** Your will be done. I live to serve—myself! Come, soldiers, come, devils, come one, come all: terror, murder, blood, rapacity, joy of joys. Come quickly; your leader calls.

Workman dressed as demons poured from the hell-mouth accompanied by smoke and thunder. They rushed among the audience, growling, snarling, yelling, making faces, threatening, accompanied by screams and laughter and yells for help. Guildsmen-actors played those parts, though local legends held that occasionally one could count more devils than actors and that on the morning following a performance the town might find itself short a guildsman or two—but then legends tend to make such claims. Just then the character of Satan appeared on the platform with a puff of grey smoke.

> **Satan:** Go, minions, do your work: bring the sinners, bring the chaste and good alike—we leave no one out. What, won't come? I'll have you yet! Hurry there—

> yes, take that one. Bring them all, jolly, jolly! Well, bring the men as well as the women: always a need for slaves. Why be a choosy mother? I'll make butter of them all!

To repel the Satan, a guildsman entered, dressed in a long cloak and sandals, to play the part of a prophet. He appeared from behind the crowd, walking in a stately gait, holding his hands palm up before him. The devils fell silent and parted, cowering, to make room for him to speak to the crowd from the base of the wagon that served as a stage.

> **Prophet:** Stop! and return whence you came, self-defiled ones. Christ will reign in a better world than this, one purged of such thoughts and such creatures. (Devils and all began to retreat, snarling and snivelling, into the hell-mouth.) Back, back Satan! You have done your evil work. No more! The true Prince comes to win back earth for God. The wheel turns; come blessed, come sinners, come all to Him, for the time nears. Come, Lord Jesu!

The crowd answered in loud calls of "Come, Lord Jesu!" They applauded and congratulated the players. Then, with the sound of thunder, the people dispersed, and a hard rain began to fall. The townsfolk dashed for cover, taking as much of their stagecraft as they could carry. As soon as the rain eased, business returned to normal: monks entered the square, singing first a dirge and then *Te Deum*. Soon after them pilgrims followed, hurried along by soldiers, who were getting tired of continually shooing the dusty wanderers out of the way of their commerce. Then once again, as the rain stopped and the folk began to gather, the acrobats renewed their show. As they danced, Abbess Hildegard, recovered at last from her illness, descended from her abbey to watch their show, accompanied by Sister Irmengard, to whom she spoke.

> **Hildegard:** Birds sing their prayers, acrobats dance theirs, even the grass bows down across the hills, swaying at God's breath and drinking the rain, praying by being. Each lives to be what it is, what God calls it to be. If only I could hear Richardis' prayers now in a drop of rain or in a gust of cool breeze, I would sing knowing that she shares and blesses our visions and our days. Like the lapwing that rises to the clouds when the sky breaks through after a storm, I rise from sickness feeling I have paid God's penance. Now I can properly mourn until I join her in the world to come.

As they stood and watched, Father Bernard of Clairvaux appeared out of the crowd to join them. Seeing him, Irmengard bowed to him and left to return to the abbey. While their talk never departed from the formal delivery required by their social positions and professions, Hildegard's and Bernard's faces shone with the light of friends addressing each other joyfully but casually.

> **Bernard:** Abbess, you yet look pale. You have been ill, as I have heard.
>
> **Hildegard:** Ill with the world's service, healed by God's.
>
> **Bernard:** So may we all be.
>
> **Hildegard:** I come here to be reconciled to the world's service as well, to see the crowds, to share their pleasure as they watch these plays and the tumbling dancers, to free myself a moment from the concerns of prayer.
>
> **Bernard:** We must live awhile in this world till we live forever in the next.

Hildegard: What brings you here, Father?

Bernard: Just now, the same thing that brings you: a moment's respite.

Hildegard: Would you hear my confession?

Bernard: You can have little to confess, you whose puissant prayers, healings and visions win the praise of common and mighty alike. What grave sins could lie upon you?

Hildegard: The worst, because the most human, our first as we rise in the morning and our last as fall asleep at night, the alpha and omega of sins: not pride, I think, but worse: doubt. No, not doubt of God—I am whole in my belief. No, doubt of God's private gift to me, which in becoming public brings doubt to public mouths and thus it returns back to private ears. I doubt a vision once its splendor fails, impaled by earthly sight. Then I believe again, when the vision mirrors the world in some forthcoming event. Worse again for me, surety replaces doubt, and then doubt returns: I doubt my prideful self as fit vessel. Cloistered in my doubt I long for this tangible truth: wind breathing in the aspens, health for the people, Richardis smiling before me.

Bernard: What gladness, this doubt of yours, that feasts you daily on both life and vision, otherwise both ignored, taken for granted. Thus doubting you submerge in the graceful flame of both, examine every particle of life, commune with the range of humanity, living at once in God's world and in God. You must know true happiness.

Hildegard: I suppose as this world offers, I do.

Bernard: Then you do, since you come from this world, and we who share it with you thank God that you do. Go on doubting, praying, healing, living, loving. Hear God's music, so you may write it or sing it, and we may marvel together. I have nothing of which to absolve you; I cannot absolve a gift. God bless you!

Hildegard: God carry you always in His music. Doubtless He does.

She waved as the great leader passed on his way. He walked, as he always did purposefully. She had no time to meditate on his words, as she was immediately greeted by another monk, whom she didn't know. He had dark, youthful, father handsome features and a serious expression. He greeted her with formal words and a reserved tone.

Guibert: Milady Abbess Hildegard?

Hildegard: Hildegard, yes, and abbess.

Guibert: I am Brother Guibert. I have been sent to help you with secretarial matters.

Hildegard: Welcome. Did you choose your work?

Guibert: I suppose I have a gift for it, for writing and recording.

Hildegard: Did you choose to work with me?

Guibert: We serve as the order and God require us.

Hildegard: Come, then, and serve God with me, since I am called to visions just as you are called to write.

Guibert: I received your letter about the shadow cast by the living fire. You truly believe in these visions?

Hildegard: They come. I speak, I preach, I compose, I heal as I can. I have faith that God will direct me right. I serve, and faith comes. I will it to come.

Guibert: You doubt, then?

Hildegard: I have no doubt that I live for God. Now, apparently, you and I will serve together for a time. Please come with me, if you will. The call has weighed heavy within me these days, and I long to record it.

Guibert: I come.

At Rupertsberg Abbey, some hours later, young Sigewize walked alone in the garden, talking, wringing her hands. In time her abbess came to offer comfort.

Sigewize: Spiritual mother, the warring voices fade from my ears. One remains, which must mean either my own or God's. Clean as a vesper bell it rings. I doubt the voice, but not the words, so I will follow them, since all else before this time floats distant as the clouds.

Hildegard: How does my young charge, bright as azaleas?

Sigewize: Better, beloved Abbess, and ever the happier in your service.

Hildegard: In God's service, Dear.

Sigewize: In both.

Hildegard: If you wish to, you may help me prepare medicines in the infirmary. Stock is low, and Sister Clementia tells me a large group of pilgrims nears our door.

Hearing them talking, Sister Keunegard fell in beside them, the fingers of her left hand playing with the hem of her robe.

Sigewize: Happily I serve God as I serve you and them.

Hildegard: Come here, dear Keunegard. I know you miss Sister Richardis as I do. What comfort does the world give us now? We must comfort each other and find blessings in the greenness of the fir trees, the call of the owl as we rise to prayer, summer sun on the hyacinths, and in the healing of God's poor of body and of spirit.

Keunegard: She has gone, and we are poor, poor.

Hildegard: We the poorer, His angels the richer.

Keunegard: She melts to dust and is gone. Oh, to be dust and gone.

Hildegard: Grieve for us, Sister, for our time without her. But we will meet her again in flesh and spirit, and when we do, we must tell her we've been humble and dutiful to God's will.

Keunegard: Meet her again. We will fly to her like birds.

Hildegard: One day, very like birds. For now, walk in the garden among the roses and lilies. They will cheer you. Sister Sigewize and I must make medicines.

Keunegard: Medicines.

Hildegard: Yes, dear, medicines, for what may be mended in this world. Walk among the angels of the garden and forget your losses in simplicity. I wish we all could.

In the Rupertsberg streets crowds milled about, as acrobats and clowns performed. A revolutionary, a man who called himself Rache, a bold, troubled young man with angry grey eyes beneath his dark, hooded cloak, climbed atop a wall and begin to call out to the folk, who listened in half-worried, half-curious silence. The age of political agitation had not yet come, but its birth was brewing. Also listening with interest, some soldiers filtered in among the folk as the speech progressed. Sister Irmengard, who had gone to town to purchase provisions, also listened intently.

> **Rache:** Townspeople, hear me. How long will you bear the oppression of the king, his magistrates and their soldiers? You raise their food, build their castles, and shovel their offal, and what do they give you for it? Grief, poverty, the stocks, the rack. And you accept it and thank them for it. And the Church: you build its proud cathedrals, and you pay it alms rather than feed your own children. They strip your bodies and flay your spirits and tell you to accept it to save your souls. Enough, Brothers and Sisters, enough! I don't tell you to fight them, openly. But you may refuse their labor, keep your alms, sabotage their buildings, and burn their engines of war. Rise up, people of God, and stand for yourselves against these demons who would in their iniquity strip you of every shred of dignity. Christians all, let us rise up against these Satans who drag you to their pits of slavery. Build your own state, your own church with God at its head, not Mammon, and you, God's true people, as its ministers!

The soldiers, unwilling to hear anymore, chased him, caught him, and, when he would not easily yield, one of them stabbed him with his sword. Once he had fallen, a second did likewise.

> **Rache:** They have killed me, who lived in God's service and yours, but others will follow me to lead you from this darkness.

> Irmengard: Stop! You will kill him.
>
> Soldier: Too late. Let him die, Sister. He is a devil.
>
> Irmengard: He is a man, however evil or misguided.
>
> Soldier: We will take him to the magistrate.
>
> Irmengard: You will take him to the abbey. Oh, if only Sister Clementia were here, you should have a time of it! Maybe the abbess can yet save his soul if not his body. Please help me here!

Recognizing the acrobats and others among the townsfolk, she enlisted their help to carry the wounded man. Several of the folk lifted him to take him to the convent. She spoke then to Damyata.

> Irmengard: Please run to Disibodenberg Abbey and get a priest. Bid him hurry.
>
> Damyata: Yes, Lady, fast as Rumor.
>
> Irmengard: When the rumor spreads, we will have soldiers and monks about us thick as flies on sour-apples.

As she left, guiding those who carried the dying man, the townsfolk congregated to whisper.

> 1st Man: Even the great lady on the hill can't save his soul. He is excommunicate.
>
> 2nd Man: What's *excommunist* mean?
>
> 1st Man: Ex-com-mun-i-cate means the church has exiled him, made him un-Christian.
>
> 2nd Man: Why would they do that?
>
> 1st Man: Blasphemy.
>
> 2nd Man: Theirs or his?

1st Man: Careful, Brother; you risk damnation.

2nd Man: The Lord made this man, right?

1st Man: The Lord made all men and women.

2nd Man: And made him Christian, right?

1st Man: Right.

2nd Man: And the Lord made the Church, which is God's folk, ergo Christian.

1st Man: Right again.

2nd Man: So how can the Church take out what God put in?

1st Man: I don't follow, but it don't sound right.

2nd Man: You must follow, or you will be damned, too. God made him Christian, so the Church, which is God's, can't make him un-Christian.

1st Man: But the man can do it himself, and the Church can know he done it.

2nd Man: If he so wills and God so wills.

1st Man: But who can tell what he wills and what God wills but God?

2nd Man: We heard him just now: "Christians all," he says. And isn't the Church's job to make Christians, not un-Christians?

1st Man: Yes, but they fear he will turn folk rebels against Church or state.

2nd Man: Do you fear him?

1st Man: Don't mind saying I do. Rebels is trouble, since who fights rebels for kings and bishops but working folk like you and me? The Church has shed him, and that's good enough for the likes of me.

2nd Man: A pot of beer says I can convince you contrariwise.

1st Man: Done.

2nd Man: Isn't St. Peter first bishop of Rome and of heaven's gate, and thus of the Church, though he did get himself excruciated upside-down?

1st Man: Ex-com-mun-i-cate: *ex* as in out, *communicate* as in speak. No, not the same thing. Or would that be excrucificate? I can't speak it out aright.

2nd Man: Speak out, you say?

1st Man: Well, yes.

2nd Man: Surely this man did speak out, and today he suffered for it like Peter and Christ. Doesn't that make him Christian?

1st Man: Depends on what he says.

2nd Man: I heard him at confession Sunday tell the priest he was ex-communi-cate before, but a priest at Bremen had absolved him for good works and made him Christian again. Our own confessor served him the Body this here Sunday. He is Christian as you, so you don't need fear him.

1st Man: Why didn't you tell me that before?

2nd Man: Because I'm thirsty and I'm broke and I want a pot of beer. Let's go!

At Rupertsberg Abbey Hildegard tended her sick, not knowing that bigger problems were making their way to her infirmary. Having given her a cold drink, she brushed the hair from the forehead of a pilgrim who lay on a bed of soft straw. She searched the face for signs she might understand and treat.

Hildegard: You may go with God now, miss, and you should feel better soon.

Pilgrim: Thank you, Lady Abbess.

Clementia: Abbess, you may not believe it, but the emperor himself has come to see you. A bit proud of himself, if you ask me.

Hildegard: I suppose at times we all are, Sisters, and none of us has the duties of an emperor. Do not keep him waiting, please. You may bring him here, Clementia.

The nuns bowed their heads as Frederick, called *Barbarossa*, entered, followed by Clementia, who cast on him and to Hildegard a look of grave distrust. The emperor gestured offhandedly to them to be at ease, but his thick, red beard bristled from his face as though in perpetual warning. Seeing the man, whose reputation sent shock waves through the empire, standing before them set even the brave Clementia on edge. Hildegard's face remained free of all expression except for the attentive, confident openness that perpetually made people both eager to speak with her and slow to depart her presence.

Frederick: Milady Abbess and our beloved friend, you need not stand on ceremony with us. Often have you sent good advice and true prophecy, and often have we prayed to God for your health and well-being. Your bishop has served tirelessly, and the counselor you warned me of has fled to Burgundy in disgrace, though, of course, I will find him. In return, I have protected and provided for Disibodenberg and Rupertsberg, assuring their safety and prosperity. Now I have come personally to you to ask a favor in return.

Hildegard: God protects us, Majesty, but you may ask what favor you will. I fear you may not like my answer.

Frederick: You will not support my candidate for pope? You will provoke a schism. Eugenius lies close to death.

Hildegard: I have no power to provoke, but I will support Alexander, the candidate of Rome. I do so not for my sake or his, but because God bids me so.

Frederick: A vision?

Hildegard: You liked my visions well enough when they served you. Now I counsel that you serve God as I do, or the cloud rising from the north will blacken the days and hearts of the German people for years to come. And you must not pursue your case against Archbishop Henry.

Frederick: Must not! I had hoped to find an ally. But I will have my way, which I believe serves the German people. Good day, Abbess. One more thing: I saw the local folk bringing in a wounded man. He is a rebel and a thief. Let him die and leave his body for the dogs. We must be stern in state as well as church. We must keep Rupertsberg safe for residents and travelers alike.

Hildegard: We may not neglect Justice any more than may the pope, lest she die upon the earth, her crown crushed, her tunic torn. I would say the same to emperor or pope; I may not be moved from God's will, as well as I can learn it. God aid Your Majesty's decisions.

Once again the nuns inclined their heads to the emperor. If he would have paid attention, he would have noticed that Sister Clementia did not bow her head.

Frederick: Do consider, milady Abbess, what powers the Church has without its secular brothers. I leave you now with the hope that you will honor my . . . request.

With a flourish and a scowl, Frederick left the infirmary. The nuns could hear him rejoin his retainers outside. They mounted their horses and rode off with purpose and confidence.

Hildegard: Such foul humors gag my breath. Can we not be rid of this petty man-squabbling and follow God? How this politics sickens my spirit. Clementia, do we have an injured man waiting?

Clementia: Just arrived and waiting the train of pomp, Abbess.

Hildegard: Bring him immediately, please.

Clementia went to the door and motioned those outside to enter. Several persons from the town entered carrying Rache, the injured revolutionary. Irmengard knelt close to him, attending desperately.

Irmengard: Soldiers stabbed him twice for preaching rebellion in the marketplace. I think he will die, but a passing priest has heard his confession and given last rites. They had feared him excommunicate, but the priest believed him Christian and reinstated him in the Church.

> Rache: My last breaths come, Abbess, but I see the way to a better world than this. Help me rise: I must meet death with my head up.
>
> Hildegard: Rest, and you may live for a time to repent your sins. If I cannot stop this bleeding, I can do nothing more but pray for you and bury you. But God shows me even now that we are right to take you in, that His angels watch over you, and that He would scourge us should we fail to give you respite.
>
> Rache: The blood comes thick and fast. I want to speak. We must not fail in our duty. The king. His bishops. Christ, save us! The sky is on fire. Warring trumpets. The fiery trumpets. God forgive me.
>
> Hildegard: Amen.

He died with his head against Hildegard's shoulder and his hand clasped in Irmengard's fingers.

> Irmengard: He saw heaven before he left this world.
>
> Hildegard: I do not know. Perhaps. But I think he found God. Has he any family?
>
> Irmengard: No one seems to know, and he would not tell me.
>
> Hildegard: Then we will have a mass sung for him and bury him on the grounds.
>
> Adelheid: Forgive me, Abbess, but I heard the king say we were to turn him out.
>
> Hildegard: We serve a higher king. We must prepare him for the holy face when we believe he died in grace.

The nuns and their servants got quickly to work, and word of Hildegard's decision soon reached Disibodenberg Abbey, to the dismay of Abbot Kuno, who paced, haranguing one of his monks.

> Kuno: I cannot rid myself of this nun, this troubling, meddlesome, disobedient sorceress, this harpy, this medusa whose molten tongue turns men's minds to stone. She will extract this heretic whom she has buried with her own hands and carry the body from this blessed ground on her back and dump it in the Rhine. She damns the very earth in which she digs.

Hildegard had anticipated that word would spread quickly, so as soon as she could, she had followed it to Kuno and had arrived in time to hear the last of his speech to his monks.

> Hildegard: All ground that receives God's children bears God's blessing, Abbot.
>
> Kuno: I will brook no equivocation or obstinacy in this matter, Abbess. The king and the archbishop have declared that the man should not receive Christian rites and burial.
>
> Hildegard: Too late: he already has.
>
> Kuno: Then the body must be exhumed and the man's memory labeled with his sins, that he may be known among the people as an example of those who flout Church and king.
>
> Hildegard: Whatever his sins, he was properly absolved and buried. Men cannot undo God's rites done, and men cannot damn what God has blessed.
>
> Kuno: You assert beyond yourself in this matter. We are consulting the Pope himself, who will undoubtedly

> concur with Frederick that holy ground will not house a heretic.

Hildegard: Heretic! He was a boy. Of what heresy is he accused?

Kuno: Defaming Church and state, doctrine and law, and of inciting the people to riot.

Hildegard: What heresy when both would oppress his soul and deny his body Christian burial?

Kuno: Will you add heresy to your own abuses of Church and privilege? You have never, since you entered my abbey, known your place. I have given in before, but in this matter, by Christ, you will serve me.

Hildegard: I will serve Christ and speak his visions, as I have always done, and I will serve you where you are right, not otherwise, despite your oaths. Beware His wrath, Abbot. He comes in a whirlwind fire, and His flaming chariot will crush you beneath its wheels.

Kuno: Threats! Once more you dare to thwart me and your Church. Take care, Abbess, for yourself and your soul, and for those of your nuns. I will have an interdiction imposed upon your convent to begin this very evening: no mass, no office, no sacraments. And it shall not be lifted until you relent and obey. Take heed: you will obey. Abbess, you may go. If you will not, I will go.

And he did. Several of Hildegard's nuns had followed her as quickly as their heels would carry them. They arrived too late to hear the argument between abbot and abbess.

Hildegard: I will obey: God and no other! We are interdicted, Beloved Ones, for now subject to the abbot in body and sense, but never in mind or spirit, where God frees the least bird in flight. Denied holy office, we may love God together and pray together. Let us do so now.

And so Kuno imposed his interdiction, and the nuns labored on without the sacraments other than those their own hearts offered. At the infirmary one everning, many days later, Irmengard and Adelheid tended a patient with Clementia standing watchfully by.

> Adelheid: How I miss the mass and the singing, the Host, the hours—especially the singing.
>
> Irmengard: We must be patient. God asks sacrifice of many, penance of most, but missing the Lord weighs the soul heavy as dusty earth.
>
> Clementia: Abbess answers to a higher source than these alb-wearing king-fearing seven-headed viper-tongued men-monsters who pretend to be the Church. The pope will clear us; you will see. She supported his election, and he knows God's word when he hears it. I have half a mind to walk to Rome myself to be sure he knows God's word when he hears it.

Once again they heard a ruckus in the hallway, and several townsfolk entered carrying Damyata, injured, with his family beside him.

> Datta: He tried to make my leap. He tried it higher than even I have. Foolish! I should have stopped him. Like his poor father. Datta must do what Datta must do, but not the poor boy.
>
> Irmengard: Clementia, help please. Adelheid: please run for the abbess. If he can be saved, she will save him.

Dall: I have lost husband; cannot now lose son. Please save him. What can mother do to save children? Storm come, earth shake, flesh weak. Even God weep.

An hour passed before Hildegard returned to the abbey, but hearing word of a new patient, she hurriedly followed Adelheid into the Infirmary.

Hildegard: Let us see. Head injury. Irmengard, bring fir sprigs, mint camphor, pork unguent mixed with strong wine, hot water and clean cloths, and do not forget the emerald shards. Being young, he glows with greenness. The years will spring from him like virile shoots if we can stay infection and get him to rest.

Adelheid: Sure, too lovely to die, he will rise anew from himself, his death but this pained sleep, his life re-christened with waking.

Dall: You believe he will live?

Adelheid: He must.

Hildegard: We will do our best. Come, pray with us. We may not have mass, but they cannot keep us from praying together. And we will minister his injuries with all our powers.

Feeling her head spin, young Sister Adelheid stumbled outside for air, and despite herself, full of worry and alone, she spoke aloud.

Adelheid: What is this grasp and whirl within me, this maelstrom that would tear heart to timbers and send it flooding into the sea? I pity the poor dark-haired youth and would draw life back to his lips. No, more than pity. God pity me for I don't know what, and keep me from sin. What sin? I will tend him as the abbess requires to make him well. And he may take long tending. His wounds cry out as silent lips cannot and call from me a life I have never known. Back now, Tears, who do not know why you fall, for sorrow or joy, since he must get well and therefore live and leave me. I will wash your wounds with fresh water, strew your room with pine, and wet your mouth with new wine. God save you, youth—and me.

At Disibodenberg Abbey Kuno fretted and stormed, but for different reasons than did Hildegard and her nuns.

Kuno: Until she relents, I can do nothing. Pleas have no use; obedience only profits.

Monk: But she insists she will see you, Milord.

Kuno: Waste of words. Well, then, send her in anyway. Once more she will be scourged.

Monk: Yes, Milord Abbot.

The monk turned to see Hildegard waiting at the door. He shrugged and waved her in.

Hildegard: Deny my visions, deny my healings, deny my abbey, but no longer deny my nuns their Christ.

Kuno: I deny? You deny. You deny! You deny your abbot, your rules, your Church, and all for nothing but your stubborn pride. Do as you are told and you will have mass this very hour. Why must you fight me at every turn? Day, night, mountain, valley, soil, water, earth, heaven, to the ninth ring of hell you thwart me, when as your abbot I guide and protect you. If only you would serve me as I would serve you. You are a noblewoman by birth, and I took you into my abbey, Jutta and I trained your thirst for the spirit, and my abbey fed and clothed the visions that bring visitors from all corners of this prison of a world to see you, you, to hear your words and beg your prayers and suffer your healings. Another abbot would have buried you as a demon alone in a silent cell to wail your prayers at the darkness. Why will you not serve me?

Hildegard: Abbot, Father Kuno: I serve God. What comes from Him I honor above earth, training, or Church. Do you think I willingly deprive my nuns of the sacraments? I do as God bids me and in doing so save them and you from God's wrath, keep them, and me, and you, in God's grace.

Kuno: How good of you to bring me God's grace.

Hildegard: We both know that hope finally rests between you and God, but I do not want to be the source of your offending, and I cannot deny His grace to me and the work He requires of me. You despise these visions as though they were mine, not His. You believe that I conjure them up to torture you, but God guides me not to your wishes or mine, but His. Do you think I love my visions? They lie upon me heavy as a shroud, burn flesh and brain till I bathe in my own ashes. They bind me above thought, above Church, above prayer, because they come from Him and not from you or me or a bishop or any earthly king.

Kuno: How do you know that they come from God? May they not as well come from the devil or some demon swimming the air for fleshly souls?

Chapter Three

Hildegard: Would a devil heal? Would a devil call me to praise and serve God? Would a devil give a poor girl the words to call people to Christ? Because you have no visions, must you assume another's come from evil rather than good?

Kuno: And how do you know they don't come from a disease of your own mind?

Hildegard: If they so persist, then my life is a disease. But even as disease they must come from God: they cast out demons and bring a young woman to Christ; they return pilgrims healed to their families; they bring king to bishop and bishop to knight with no intention of profit, each blessing each, all praising God, squaring off the corners of the earth in peace. And they keep the scourge of God from your abbey when you would exhume dead war from its silent plot.

Kuno: Will you never relent? No, you shall relent. This time no bishop, no pope aids you, no misbegotten miracle misleads authority to support your tangent cause. Will you not give up this vision when authorization lies distant as some Cathayan skiff moored in a windless harbor?

Hildegard: What comes from the Author of all flesh transcends fleshly authorization.

Kuno: Surely you are some curse sent to try me Job-like in my faith. Will you give me no peace until the angel rip the skin from my bones and crush them to dust?

Hildegard: God gives trials. God gives peace.

Kuno: You argue like a scholar.

Hildegard: I do not want to argue at all. I do not even want the visions. But because they come, I must do my duty to God as you must to your Church and flock. Abbot, please, will you serve mass to my nuns?

Kuno: Will you relent? No, I did not think so. I will not, not till the interdiction is lifted from above.

Hildegard: Even now God lifts it. I can see it pass like a blackbird rising from a corpse awaking dove-like from beneath black wings as the fire of morning presses life between its lips. Not long will my nuns suffer now.

Kuno: You dream.

One of Kuno's attending monks entered silently. He coughed gently, interrupting their silence.

Monk: Pardon, Milord Abbot, a letter.

Kuno: From where?

Monk: Rome, Milord.

Kuno: Whom?

Monk: The Pope, Milord.

Kuno: Here then, you, listen. No, no, Brother Gabriel, remain, and let us hear the contents together. Ahem. Dear Abbot, yes yes, certain correspondences, regarding the buried revolutionary, yes . . . not to be exhumed . . . Christian conversion when . . . last rites . . . miracle—no it may not be!—the interdiction to be lifted as of this writing, to be carried out immediately upon receipt . . . and mass sung. . . . Angels and devils, it galls me! Shall my word carry no coin, nor the bishop nor the archbishop guide Rome to its own interest? Am I of no account? From the rampant bear to the tearful pleiades, may God cut a hole in the sky and suck me through to heaven or oblivion, so I am no longer thrall to the mad and weak-willed. Let me run naked, preaching to the thorns and brambles, my feet tilling and my own blood feeding the earth, till, wizened, I shrivel and dissolve in the wind, just so I am no longer subject to a woman's whim and the unctuous guile of office.

As he concluded, Hildegard felt her mind filled with a vision. It began as a burst of light and pain, then took shape for her thoughts alone.

Hildegard: Woe to the wretched who believe God a deceiver. Oh Fear of God, clench us like a hammer to your breast, wield us as tools to raise from these elements a bridge to Heaven. Fear God, fear God, till our necks crane and our hair humbles in the dust.

Kuno: Dust. You do not know dust. What! You see one now, do you not, woman? You see with His eyes in your heart. Does He burn you? Do you suffer with Him, for Him? Tell me. What else do you see? Speak!

Hildegard: Capernaum, you will not see heaven. Antichrist shall shake aside the fire and blood in his chains, and the serpent will glorify the dust, till the elements twine about him. Yes, Jutta, like you we will die and rise again with Him, the reassembled shards of His flaming sword, our voices thunder, our eyes lightning, to strike down the devil.

Kuno: Jutta, here? Is she speaking? What does she say to me?

Hildegard: Blood, bone, breath, soul, the elements of Christ brought by Mary and paid to God so we may hear the greening of the great voice and, shaped to God, shoot like stars at His touch.

Kuno: Have we paid God? Sister? Does He hear us in our sin? Jutta, what does she say? Fear is not enough. Tell me. I must know more. Sister!

Hildegard: Forgive me, Abbot. I am spent.

Kuno: Does the voice of God ring and die so suddenly? Does He rain a drop when oceans would leave us parched? More: I must have more! I must see, must hear, must feel. Tell me how.

Hildegard: I do not know how. There is no *how*. He comes or does not come. I have nothing to do with it other than to hear and to listen and remember.

Kuno: So I see: weak, numb, voiceless. Oh, I would make a stronger vessel. I would shout the day long and dance the world askew with telling His word. I would not tire till the sun and moon struck the bottom of the sea and bounced earth from the heavens, toppling it like a child's ball into the abyss.

Hildegard: He calls whom He will. Strength, office, age, place, race, sex—no matter.

Kuno: Abbess: you may return to your convent. I will serve mass myself in an hour. Earth cover me in its shroud.

As Hildegard began to speak, he waved her words aside and left her, shaking his head.

Hildegard: Thank you, Abbot. Long after summer pales, winter ends fall's flight. When day blooms, day dies in another's night. God bless Kuno and us.

Brother Gabriel: Amen.

Hildegard: Brother, will you help me to my abbey? I feel weak.

When she had returned home, Hildegard remained abed for two days, her body in pain and her mind swimming in visions. When she awoke, she had Clementia call for Brother Guibert, who brought with him writing materials.

Hildegard: Brother, I have several visions to record. Please write them, leaving space for explication, to which we'll return once you have recorded them all. They have long urged me, and I must clear my thoughts of them so that I may heal.

Guibert: Go on, Milady Abbess. I await your dictation.

Hildegard: Thank you, brother. First, I saw a man, his feet spread slightly but set firmly upon the ground at the edge of the sea, his shoulders stretching above the clouds, his head to the sky. He faced east. His hair fell to his shoulders, and his arms stretched to the north and south. His face flashed blue-bright in a serious expression. At his mouth a cloud formed into the shape of a trumpet, which he took in his hand and from which he blew three long, fiery, luminous notes. From one of the notes emerged a cloud, and in the cloud lived a bright multitude of faces. They held before them a winged tablet with a title inscribed in red letters: "The Wisdom from God." They read from the tablet together, and their voices rose like the song of angels. From that cloud fled a second cloud, thick and dark, which had grown from the second trumpet note. In it dwelt ashen faces, and a voice rose from one of them, speaking "Deceiver." That cloud, caught in a wind from the trumpet, rushed into the abyss. A third cloud, emerging from the third note, grew bright and luminous, and it encompassed the sun and the moon, setting them on either side of the man. A voice spoke from the cloud: "Christ has brought light to the world, and His Church shall reflect His light even into the darkness." Then another cloud approached from the north and took the shape of a serpent. From its mouth spilled a torrent of smoke. It rose toward the face of the man, as if to cover it. But the sun shone down on it and dissolved it into shadows that slunk off into the abyss, and the sun spoke, "Light will always pierce the darkness for those who watch and listen." And the moon said, "Speak out this vision, as the Living Light commands." Oh. I feel better, having spoken it, but now I tire again. I must try to go on; just let me get a breath. Next came a fire-red head with long, white wings. Sorry, I must pause a moment.

Guibert: Astonishing! The vividness and detail.

Hildegard: You remind me of Brother Volmar when you say that.

Guibert: You miss him?

Hildegard: I do.

Guibert: I will endeavor to record as honestly and faithfully as he did.

Hildegard: You give me great comfort.

Guibert: But please tell me, how do you know how much of the vision comes from God, how much from you, and how much from . . . .

Hildegard: Brother, please don't say that. At best I trust that they come from God, at worst that they come from me. I can't divide a vision into parts that I trust and parts I don't. I write or speak what I see, and I have faith that God gives the vision to me and hope that I recall it as he wishes. I do my best to vary nothing. Sometimes, with Volmar, I couldn't even remember what I had spoken, only that I had. You understand why I must rely on my scribe's diligence.

Guibert: I do, sister. But what then of your letters that come as praise or blame, directive or advice, rather than as visions that prophesy?

Hildegard: There I speak also as God leads me. As Father he makes me kind and rational; as Mother he makes me strong and firm; as Sibling he makes me open and compassionate. I have for so long heard the words and seen the images that I have learned gradually to trust the gift and live up to its responsibility. How do you know, brother, that you record my words correctly, that you spell what others can read and understand? You trust your training and the skills God has allotted you. How does a smith trust his tongs or a wheelwright his hammer? For years I fought the gift, trying to subdue it within myself, until I thought my head would split. As I spoke, God gave me relief. I believe we have little choice but to find the gifts within ourselves and use them such as they are: a blessing to find, a curse to ignore, as in the proverb of the talents.

> Guibert: You say, finally, that we must allow ourselves to become what God made us. I find no great revelation in that.
>
> Hildegard: Neither do I, Brother, though once, afraid to speak, I did speak. The world does not deal kindly with those who speak out, and a tithe—I am no more than a tithe, you know—has little hope to serve as God's vessel to the world.
>
> Guibert: Yet I long to hear more of the visions.
>
> Hildegard: And I to tell them. Shall we continue?
>
> Guibert: Let's do, if you feel well enough.
>
> Hildegard: I feel old and wearier than ever I have, but at the same time eager to speak.
>
> Guibert: And I more than ever feel eager to write, though the fingers cramp.
>
> Hildegard: The task is to find the calling, then follow it, as the notes follow the strumming of the strings. Whatever comes that has value comes from that drive and from His kindness.
>
> Guibert: You were speaking before something about a red head with white wings?
>
> Hildegard: Ah yes, I was. . . .

Some days later at the Rupertsberg Abbey Infirmary, two young people sat talking as at such an age we naturally do, and after such a fashion as had over the past days grown particularly to please them. They had found themselves often thrown together, and their acquaintace had grown from hesistancy to eager conversation to the point where eyes meet and lock and, though cheeks blush, they refuse any more coyness.

Adelheid: I was born here, raised here, I serve God here, and I will die here. Tell me about the mountains where you were born. I love mountains.

Damyata: Mountains like you never see: blue in the red dawn they push sun out of river's pink haze and kiss it on its way, then catch it in west again to lay it quietly to night's rest.

Adelheid: Awfully forward, these mountains of yours.

Damyata: Stay, and I will tell you how the rivers drop in gorges white as icicles, melting from snow that sits white as a bishop's hat on the peaked mountains.

Adelheid: Not *hat, miter.*

Damyata: Miter, hat, no matter. Snow white as your skin, mountains blue and deep as your eyes. Why you do not marry?

Adelheid: I am married, to Christ.

Damyata: Yes, truly, but have you never thought of husband, children, love?

Adelheid: I love God.

Damyata: Truly so, but have you never loved a man?

Adelheid: Of course not. I am still a girl myself.

Damyata: Not girl, woman. Beautiful young woman.

Adelheid: If I am beautiful, it is because I love God.

Damyata: Because God love you and has make you beautiful.

Adelheid: What about you? Do you love God?

Damyata: I love God though He let my father die. I love God for my family. I love God for dancing. I love

God for birds and mountains and bread and cheese and wine and shoes for winter, when I have them, and daisies—you like daisies?

Adelheid: Love them.

Damyata: And bees heavy with . . . what word? I don't know the word. With what they use to make honey. For Mother's eyes when she speaks of Father, for the people's faces when we dance, and for you . . .

Adelheid: For me? Why?

Damyata: You never thought of husband?

Adelheid: I am a nun. I made a vow to God.

Damyata: Never?

Adelheid: When I was small I had a dream that a dark-haired young man would ride up on a horse. He would dance with me, and we would ride off together to a bright, colorful kingdom and live happily ever after. We would dance and dance, all the way down the hill, through a field of flowers, and disappear, sailing down the river.

Damyata: He has come here, the young man. No prince, and he have no horse. The river is life. He is here, if you want him. Maybe God sent dream, and God sends man, and you serve by living dream.

Adelheid: You're barely a man, and I am merely a girl.

Damyata: Your reasons say no, but heart says yes.

Adelheid: How do you know that? You are no prophet.

Damyata: Don't know. I had dream in my sickness of a woman who reached into my grave to pull me out.

> She was young and strong and beautiful and had eyes like mountains. She was you.

Adelheid: How could you know that?

Damyata: I see, I feel, I believe. I believe, I know not why, that God has given you a vision and me a vision. I believe, do not know why, that we must have faith in vision, whatever it teaches us. Rock, river, earth, sun: what do they mean if we have not vision? I believe you love me.

Adelheid: No. What can I do if I do?

Damyata: What you must, if you love me, and what you want. The world runs past, the great wheel turns, and we, like children's toys, spin, fall, and are forgotten. Come with me. Will you come with me? I owe life to you, and I love you. Will you come?

Adelheid: No. Yes. Where will we go?

Damyata: We will go. I have family. We are young. We will live. We will travel. We will dance. We will go now to find priest.

Adelheid: I don't know. Oh, let's go before I know. Now, I believe. Let's go while I believe.

After Adelheid had drawn the headcover from her habit and thrown a cloak over her shoulders, an unexpected guest, striding toward them, spoke, intruding on their thoughts.

Bernard: Young woman, what are you doing here?

Adelheid: I serve the nuns.

Bernard: Young man, you two should not be alone here.

Damyata: I have been in sick room many days. They have saved my life, the nuns of the great lady. Young woman now shows me way out.

Adelheid: I am going with him—to show him the way.

Bernard: Be quick, then.

Hmmm, Bernard said to himself as they hurriedly left. Bernard stood but a moment with his own thoughts. Hildegard appeared along the pathway and greeted him.

Hildegard: Father?

Bernard: Abbess, the love of God dresses you like a gown.

Hildegard: Welcome always, Father and Friend. The Pope has lifted our interdiction, and you may share mass with us directly.

Bernard: You have friends in high places.

Hildegard: The highest, I hope and believe. Did you see a young man here? I had come to check on him.

Bernard: Yes, a young man and a young woman, they left together.

Hildegard: Left? A nun?

Bernard: I am not sure, but perhaps . . .

Hildegard: She has gone with him. Dear God, Adelheid, how could you? Perhaps you were meant so. You seemed too much the butterfly for this quiet life. God forgive and bless both. Had I paid more attention, I would have seen it–but then perhaps I did see it, saw it as right in its way, and let it go.

Bernard: May God then bless them and us.

Hildegard: Shall we go to mass, Father? Maybe first a walk in the garden.

Bernard: And a prayer.

Hildegard: Always.

In the Rupertsberg streets folk mingled in the marketplace. Monks passed on their rounds, singing their *Miserere*, and departed. Nuns entered, singing from the *Ordo Virtutum*, the song about the Martyrs, then they too passed on their way. The acrobats entered, accompanied by Damyata and Adelheid, who for the first but not last time danced with them.

As they danced, Keunegard sat on the hill above and watched her lost sister. Inside, her thoughts turned like pinwheels; outside, her lips mumbled incomprehensibly. As the performance concluded, Damyata and Adelheid bade good-byes to family and crowd, exited to the congratulations of the townsfolk. New strains of music rose from the crowd, but Keunegard stood absorbed in her own thoughts, speaking aloud to herself.

Keunegard: Serpents, slitherers, out of the clouds. Sins cradle smoke from the stars, and the foul fire drips to scorch the earth. All three: the first a white shroud in a white shroud in a black shroud. She is long gone, remains alone, but not alone. The second still glows in the dark. Her stay was too short, but she remains, too. The third walks in the light, but has leaped into darkness. Alas, she is gone, gone. The martyrs must redeem them all and bring them back to us. Flesh for flesh, blood for blood. I have waited. I will give my blood now.

As Keunegard edged toward the sharp brink of the hillside, Hildegard, who had been searching, spotted her and called out.

Hildegard: Sister, what are you doing? Keunegard, be careful. Please come down!

Keunegard: Down, down. All go down. The dove swoops, the cross falls, the fly dies in its flesh, the spirit comes, goes, and all flesh dies. Angels will raise them up.

Hildegard: Sister, you are too close to the edge. Do not try to come down. Just step back and wait for me. I will come for you!

Keunegard: I will come down to raise them up, like Him. Devils, back. I burn for His glory and fly with His spirit. Save us, Christ. I am the smoke blown from the censer. My blood will dissolve the stones and raise them crying. Crying. Look! The dove. The dove!

Hildegard screamed as Keunegard leapt from the hillside onto the rocks below.

※ ※ ※

Two days later, outside Rupertsberg, the nuns gathered at a crossroads where some townsmen had dug Keunegard's grave.

Clementia: Christ will forgive her.

Irmengard: She committed a mortal sin.

Clementia: I do not believe it for an instant.

Irmengard: She committed suicide before a crowd of people.

Clementia: I will not believe it. She was sick and did not know what she did.

Irmengard: I hope you are right. Abbess, you were there.

Hildegard: The Church has made its judgment. In our hearts we may believe as we will.

As they spoke, Kuno entered at a distance, a cowl covering his features.

Irmengard: What do you believe?

Hildegard: Sister Keunegard was not like us. She bore a special burden and endured a special grace.

Irmengard: Do you think she was a prophet?

Hildegard: She suffered as long as she could, and I could not cure her. She was not for this world. I wish only that we could have buried her at the abbey rather than at this dingy crossroads.

Sigewize: Was she a martyr?

Hildegard: She was unfortunate, and so are we, to have lost her.

Irmengard: But she is damned, I fear. Are suicides not damned?

Hildegard: So we believe. We must believe her death an accident, caused by demon or disease, because we loved her. And we must pray for her.

Irmengard: Have you no vision now? You did not argue with the abbot or the bishop about the burial. Can we petition? Can we do nothing?

Clementia: We can pray for her and for ourselves.

Hildegard: Oh, Sister, why does vision fail me when I would save your soul for Christ? Christ, how have I failed you that I lack vision to save a soul?

Irmengard: You saved a thief and rebel; can you find no way to save a servant of God?

> Hildegard: The mountain opens to spout fire when the heat rises; the lion tears its prey when God says *hunger*. Lightening rips the oak, hooves cleave the dust, swords open the breast till the soul runs out to cover the earth. Is her blood not enough? Is His blood not enough to save her? And no vision to relieve my own bleeding or the hearts of my children? Must I fail them when they need me?
>
> Irmengard: Abbess, you have done what you can. So have we. Let us go home now.
>
> Hildegard: No, not yet—please go without me. I will come along soon. I must think and pray, find a way to fill the space vision has abandoned.

They departed, leaving Hildegard and Sigewize together beside the grave and Kuno hidden behind.

> Hildegard: Even the abbot pitied me this time, I think. Nor could he do anything. The law is clear, but my heart speaks otherwise. A troubled soul, a child's mind: she had no judgment, no understanding of right, wrong, law, rule, testament, warning. She knew suffering and love and sacrifice. Is that not enough? Tell me, oh my Christ?

Even Kuno had nothing to say. He bowed his head, sighed heavily, and walked away.

> Sigewize: Abbess: God will forgive her. She was mad, and God must forgive madness, right? I know about madness. And I know that she loved me. God rewards love, Abbess?
>
> Hildegard: We are all mad till the world ends. Go home, child, and do not fear for her or yourself.

Sigewize: I will pray for her and for me and for you.

Hildegard: Do you feel well enough to leave me for a bit? Thank you, dear one.

Hildegard stood in silent prayer for some time. When she walked tiredly up the road on her way home, she found before her, waiting by the gate of her abbey, a cowled figure.

Kuno: I needed to say something. I am sorry about your nun.

Hildegard: Yes.

Kuno: There was nothing I could do. Church law is clear.

Hildegard: Nothing you could do. Thank you, Abbot.

Kuno: You have never understood responsibility. I stand with you, but what you want does not matter. What I want does not matter. We believe in the Church and we follow the Church. Our life is the Church.

Hildegard: And we hide behind the Church when we need it to protect us from our fears.

Kuno: Once again you condemn me.

Hildegard: I condemn the times that produce men who cannot stand up to false rulings and foolish rulers for the sake of those they love and for the weak of body, mind, or spirit who need their protection.

Kuno: You think I wanted this to happen? What do you want me to do?

Hildegard: As you said, what we want does not matter. We must follow the voice of God when we hear it.

Kuno: And you know the voice of God when you hear it, so I should follow you.

Hildegard: I am not asking you to do anything but leave me to my grief.

Kuno: I must return to my abbey, and you should do the same. Maybe you can keep the remainder of your nuns from falling.

Hildegard: Yes. Please do go, Abbot.

Kuno: You are stubborn as the devil. The law says you grieve for the lost.

Hildegard: And perhaps for what we never had.

Kuno: Only believe me: this time I suffer with you.

Hildegard: I know. I am sorry, truly. Thank you.

The abbot left her again, but when Hildegard raised her eyes, another figure, a young woman, stood before her. Hildegard also noticed a young man standing behind a tree not far away, listening intently.

Adelheid: Abbess, forgive me.

Hildegard: Only God's forgiveness finally matters, child. But I can love, and so can you, and we must love Him first and one another as well.

Adelheid: I do love Christ, Abbess.

Hildegard: You don't need to call me "Abbess" now; you may call me "Hildegard" or "Friend."

Adelheid: Abbess, Friend, Mother, I fear I caused this, with sister. Will you forgive and bless me?

Hildegard: God bless us both and poor Sister Keunegard. You could not cause what the world made inevitable.

Adelheid: She scared me, but I always loved her. What will you do?

Hildegard: Mourn.

Adelheid: Do you mourn for me, too?

Hildegard: I regret broken vows and the Church's loss of one of Christ's own. But tell me, do you believe you've done the right thing?

Adelheid: I believe Christ called me to marry Damyata. Can I still serve God in my marriage?

Hildegard: We serve, I suppose, by faith and by quick devotion to His calling, whatever it may be. What about the young man?

Damyata: A thousand pardons, Abbess: I love her.

Hildegard: You must seek your pardon from Christ, who asks no penance for love, only for sin.

Adelheid: Have I sinned?

Hildegard: You have given up one vow for another. See that you keep it and love him all the days of your life. And you, young man: you have taken Adelheid from God's house. See that you love and protect her and return her to Christ betimes. You have seen a priest?

Adelheid: Yes, of course, Mother.

Hildegard: Then go together in God's law. Love each other, and sow that love in Christ's field, so you may one day harvest it together in Heaven.

Together Adelheid and Damyata thanked her, and they kissed her hands. Arm in arm, the couple left.

Hildegard watched Adelheid and Damyata depart, then renewed her journey on tired legs, trudging up the hill to the abbey with her eyes downcast. When she reached the abbey gate, Kuno stood there waiting for her, as if to speak to her. He stopped himself, blessed her with the sign of the Cross, and made his own way home. Hildegard stood alone at the gate, watching the stars rising.

> Hildegard: Young, they hardly notice the cruelty of the world. May they learn no more of it than they know now, till death cover them, and may love recover them to Christ at the world's end, when the horses of the night lick stars from the hand of heaven, and the flesh-clotted teeth of the beast dissolve in the last great fire before the world and Heaven are one. And you, beloved Sister Keunegard, what can I offer you in my prayers? Lord, forgive young Adelheid, and me if I have misled her, and, Keunegard, forgive me if I did not hear your cry. As long as I remain among his living lights, I will kneel on your grave and pray each day, singing silent office for your soul, or, if duty keep me, I will kneel in what dust I can find and mingle with the earth that holds you. The young Rache had a vision of justice in this world, our Adelheid of love in this world; you too, Sister, had a vision, not unlike mine, and in your suffering you followed it as you could. I pray it led you to merciful God. Are all His gifts so terrible? What's this? What pitying hand reaching from the nighted clouds to lift you from your grief-shattered bones? I pray it is, oh, how I pray God save you! May I in my dust and tears be raised up with you, whole as earth has never seen us, that we may meet on the right hand of God. Good-bye, my dear. When vision ends, may love's wisdom count us blessed, and may angels' assurance sing us all to rest.

The cool shadow of evening fell then even as it does now, and Hildegard sought a cold supper, such as she might still find on the larder at her abbey. She arranged in her thoughts the prayers that should accompany her until evensong, hoping they would last that long and that her strength would last as long as she needed it.

❧ ❧ ❧

Blessed Hildegard of Bingen continued writing, preaching, healing, composing, and serving the Church and her community until she died in 1179 at the age of eighty-one. *Bene vixit; bene decessit.*

Hildegard's Writings

MYSTICAL WORKS

> *Scivias*
> *Liber Vitae Meritorum*
> *Liber Civinorum Operum*

MEDICAL WORKS

> *Physica*, or *Liber Simplicis Medicinae*
> *Causae et Curae*, or *Liber Compositae Medicinae*

MUSICAL WORKS

> *Symphonia Harmoniae Caelestium Revelationum*
> *Ordo Virtutum*

ON HER OWN PRIVATE LANGUAGE

> *Lingua Ignota* and *Litterae Ignota*

EXEGETICAL WORKS

> *Expositio Evangeliorum*
> *Vita St. Disibod*
> *Vita St. Rupert*

LETTERS

Selected Secondary Bibliography

THE READER interested in information and opinions about Hildegard's life and work will find an ever-expanding array of books and articles, some intensely scholarly, some designed more for general appeal. The following list offers only a place to start, some books and articles that I found particularly helpful in my own research to write this short book.

Anderson, Bonnie S., and Judith P. Zinsser. *A History of Their Own: Women in Europe from Prehistory to the Present.* Vol. 1. New York: Harper & Row, 1988.
Flanagan, Sabina. *Hildegard of Bingen, 1098–1179: A Visionary Life.* London and New York: Routledge, 1989.
Fox, Matthew, O.P., ed. *Illuminations of Hildegard of Bingen.* Sante Fe: Bear & Co., 1985, 2002.
Hildegard of Bingen. *Scivias.* Trans. Bruce Hozeski. Sante Fe: Bear & Co., 1986.
Hollister, C. Warren. *Medieval Europe: A Short History.* 4th ed. New York: John Wiley & Sons, 1978.
Newman, Barbara. *Sister of Wisdom: St. Hildegard's Theology of the Feminine.* Berkeley, Los Angeles, London: U of California P, 1987.
Newman, Barbara, editor. *Voice of the Living Light: Hildegard of Bingen and Her World.* Berkeley: U of California Press, 1998.
Scholz, Bernhard W. "Hildegard von Bingen on the Nature of Woman." *American Benedictine Review* 31 (1989): 361–83.
Sur, Carolyn Wörman. *The Feminine Images of God in the Visions of Saint Hildegard of Bingen's Scivias.* Lewiston, NY: Edwin Mellen, 1993.
Sweet, Victoria. "Hildegard of Bingen and the Greening of Medieval Medicine." *Bulletin of the History of Medicine* 73 (1999): 381–403.
Thiebaux, Marcelle, ed. and trans. *The Writings of Medieval Women: An Anthology.* 2nd. ed. New York: Garland, 1994.
Weeks, Andrew. *German Mysticism from Hildegard of Bingen to Ludwig Wittgenstein: A Literary and Intellectual History.* Albany: State University of New York Press, 1993.

www.ingramcontent.com/pod-product-compliance
Lightning Source LLC
Chambersburg PA
CBHW072155160426
43197CB00012B/2392